THE JOY OF BECOMING

It's not how you get there,
It's how you grow there.

Special <u>FREE</u> Bonus Gift for You

To help you achieve more success, get your
FREE BONUS RESOURCE at:

www.TheMariaCollins.com

Download the Fast Action Workbook that accompanies this book to help you clarify your vision, experience freedom, and live with Passion, Purpose, and Prosperity.

MARIA COLLINS®

Copyright © 2023 Maria Collins.

ALL RIGHTS RESERVED. No part of this book or its associated ancillary materials may be reproduced or transmitted in any form or by any means, electronic or mechanical, including photocopying, recording, or by any informational storage or retrieval system without permission from the publisher. PUBLISHED BY: Maria Collins, DISCLAIMER AND/OR LEGAL NOTICES.

Scripture taken from the New King James Version®. Copyright © 1982 by Thomas Nelson. Used by permission. All rights reserved.

Scriptures taken from the Holy Bible, New International Version®, NIV®. Copyright © 1973, 1978, 1984, 2011 by Biblica, Inc.™ Used by permission of Zondervan. All rights reserved worldwide. www.zondervan.com The "NIV" and "New International Version" are trademarks registered in the United States Patent and Trademark Office by Biblica, Inc.®

ISBN: 9798366498623

Independently Published

Visit us at: www.themariacollins.com

WHAT OTHERS ARE SAYING ABOUT MARIA COLLINS, HER STORY, & STRATEGIES

"The book you're holding in your hand, "The Joy of Becoming" is just that, becoming the best you that you can be for God. There are people who write books, and then there are people who the book, reflects who they are becoming. Maria shares very personal stories of her journey to be the best wife, mother, and her desire to help others win in life. She doesn't just share her wins, but she shares how she faced the challenges and overcame them. When you read someone else's book, you're reading, the best part of them and the gift that God created them to be on earth. God desires for you to become the best that you can be for him and this is a resource that will help you do just that."

-**Sheila Craft**, Pastor, Author & Speaker

"Maria's story will inspire you to clarify your purpose and pursue your dreams like never before."

-**Vickie Flowers**, Marriage and Family Pastor at Elevate Life Church

"Maria encourages you in enjoying the journey of becoming ready to receive the blessings God has for you and providing you with practical advice that has the power to transform your life. "

-**Megan Unsworth**, Cofounder of Life on Fire

Cast a Vision

"Read this book and follow Maria's strategies to become your best self and live your best life!"

-**James Malinchak**, Featured on ABC's hit TV show "Secret Millionaire" • Best-selling Author, *"Millionaire Success Secrets"* • Founder, www.BigMoneySpeaker.com

"Maria Collins understands the heart of the female entrepreneur and the delicate work/life balance and unexpected ruts we can all fall into with our thinking and habits. Her book, The Joy of Becoming, reads like an encouraging how-to from your best friend. Not only will you feel seen and understood, but you'll also be challenged. Whether you're looking to make small changes or make a major shift in your life, Maria will give you the tools you need to reinvent yourself. Get ready to become more than you dream possible!"

-**Jessica Gilliam**, M.S., Branding Coach • Founder of BLACKSTONE DIGITAL Marketing and Consulting

MOTIVATE AND INSPIRE OTHERS!
"Share This Book"

Retail $18.97

Special Quantity Discounts

5-20 Books	$16.97
21-99 Books	$14.97
100-499 Books	$12.97
500-999 Books	$10.97
1,000+ Books	$8.97

To Place an Order Contact:
Email: coachmariacollins@gmail.com
www.TheMariaCollins.com

THE IDEAL PROFESSIONAL
Speaker
FOR YOUR NEXT EVENT!

Any organization that wants to develop its people to become "extraordinary" needs to hire Maria Collins for a keynote and/or workshop training!

TO CONTACT OR BOOK
MARIA COLLINS
TO SPEAK:

Email: coachmariacollins@gmail.com
www.TheMariaCollins.com

THE IDEAL *Coach* FOR YOU!

If you're ready to overcome challenges, have major breakthroughs, and achieve higher levels of success, then you will love having Maria Collins as your coach!

TO CONTACT
MARIA COLLINS

Email: coachmariacollins@gmail.com
www.TheMariaCollins.com

Dedication

It is with honor, respect, and appreciation that I dedicate this book to my wonderful family. Without your support, love, and example throughout my life, I would not be where I am today. I'm so grateful for each one of you. Thank you! I love you so much!

Edson Carneiro (Dad)

Marlene Carneiro (Mom)

James Collins (Husband)

Zoey Collins (Daughter)

Noah Collins (Son)

Maria Beatriz, Maria Izabel, and Maria Fernanda (Sisters)

Table of Contents

Introduction _____ x

PART I: Dream of the Life You Want to Live!

1. Cast a Vision _____ 1

2. Be Specific _____ 13

3. Find What Matters Most _____ 23

4. Establish Core Values _____ 29

5. Know Your "Why" _____ 39

PART II: Assessing The Life You Have

6. Take Inventory _____ 46

7. Navigating Every Season _____ 62

8. Declutter Your Life _____ 75

PART III: Your Path to New Life

9. Your Identity _____ 89

10. Renew Your Mind _____ 108

11. Finding Your Joy _____ 118

12. Design Your Rhythm _____ 128

Introduction

As a kingdom builder, author, speaker, and personal and business coach, my mission is to empower, motivate and teach women how to realize their God-given potential and thrive in the life God intends for them to live. As a constant learner and lover of Jesus and self-development, I can confidently say that the practical and results-oriented guidance contained in this book will improve and transform your life if you let it. I will help you grow closer in your relationship with God and boost your confidence to step into new levels of success spiritually, personally, and professionally.

Prepare to experience life like never before through a fresh perspective, a persistent focus on all the blessings and beauty around you, an abundance mentality, and a new level of freedom, fulfillment, and joy. This can mean improving your health, happiness, relationships, self-care, and overall quality of life, or any specific area you want to improve in your life.

Introduction

Living a life with God in the center of everything has been proven repeatedly to empower anyone to overcome any challenge, experience peace, freedom, and breakthrough, and turn any circumstance around in unexpected ways. Whether you're looking to create a small change or a total life transformation, you have found the right book at the right time for you. No coincidence; just God doing His thing!

You are about to begin a transformational journey using God's way which is guaranteed to shift anything in your life. This method has transformed many lives around the world, including my own, and it just might be what you have been waiting for to transform yours as well. An ancient Chinese proverb says, "When the student is ready, the teacher will appear." I believe God has led you to this book for a reason, and my prayer is that the Holy Spirit would speak to you through the words He has given me in this book. It is my honor to be used as God's vessel to share what He has done in and through my life so I can live the abundant life He has planned for me and empower you to do the same. I have been obedient to God's guidance to ensure this book will be a life-transforming investment of your time, energy, and

Introduction

devotion. Thank you for allowing me to be part of your life and opening your heart for God to perform His wonderful work in you. An amazing journey is about to begin, and God will be by your side each step of the way. I will be here as well to support and cheer you along the way.

With love,

Maria Collins

PART I

Dream of the Life
You Want to Live

1. Cast a Vision

Casting a vision of the life you want to live is as simple as thinking or imagining and writing down what you want your life to look like. I always like to seek the Word of God to begin anything of importance, because His Word is a guidepost that directs you toward the truth and helps you understand the path He wants you to take in life. This scripture from the book of Habakkuk speaks to not only the importance of creating a vision for your life, but also the significance of writing that vision down:

> *"Then the Lord answered me and said: "Write the vision and make it plain on tablets, that he may run who reads it."*
>
> Habakkuk 2:2 (NKJV)

Cast a Vision

The basic fact is that you create the meaning of your life, and that meaning gives purpose to your life. Without meaning and purpose, you would not exist. If you woke up today with breath in your lungs, then you can rest assured that God still has a plan and purpose for you on Earth. God created you uniquely for a purpose; a purpose no one else can fulfill but you.

God has great plans for your life. His plans are good, filled with hope and plenty of the good things in life. The desires God has planted in your heart are yours. He created you in his image: wonderful and beautiful in your own way!

> *"For I know the plans I have for you," declares the Lord, "plans to prosper you and not to harm you, plans to give you hope and a future."*
> Jeremiah 29:11 (NIV)

THE JOY OF BECOMING

When you choose to live your life following His Word and in obedience to His commands, He will deliver to you more than you could ever ask or imagine; not because of who you are and what you have done, but because of who He is and His unfailing love for you, His child!

When I first started thinking and dreaming about my future family, I tried to think about every aspect of what I wanted that family to look like. I wanted us to love and cherish each other. I would have an amazing husband and kids, and we would love to spend time together, travel together, and have so much fun! However, as I grew up, experienced life, and watched the world around me, I started allowing the world to influence my thoughts and beliefs. Somehow, I lost focus on my deep desires and the things I wanted for my future and slipped into living my life by default. I found myself trying to control every aspect of my life, but without a clear direction for where my life was headed. I thought if I had control, I could make everything happen on my own.

As I look back on the love relationships I had before marriage, I was often overlooking red flags about the other person and my gut feeling telling me that things would not turn out the way I wanted. I was always trying to make it work. To *force* it to work. I thought I could change the other person. I didn't want to let go because deep inside I was afraid I would not have another chance to find love, so every relationship became critical. I had to make *that* relationship work out. Not only was this a poor strategy for developing the kind of relationship that would stand the test of time, but it also put undue pressure on those relationships and created unrealistic expectations.

I'm sure most readers can relate to wanting so badly for something to happen *right now* that you try to take control of the situation and ignore all the signs showing you it is not the right thing for you. I certainly have, and I'm still a work in progress when it comes to releasing control of situations and giving God control, and trusting Him to work all things together for my good and His glory. Understanding when it is time to act and when it is time to let go and let God do His work is one of the most important lessons I've had to learn.

In November 2012, I had had enough of the wrong relationships and the pain that came with them.

THE JOY OF BECOMING

I was done making the wrong choices regarding my love life. One night in my room I had a real conversation with God. I asked for forgiveness of my sins, and I surrendered all to Him. I had come to the end of myself, I could not do it on my own, and I gave Him control to bring the right man into my life. After that, I knew this was the right step. I could *feel* it. Things started to shift in my heart and love life. I was set free from the weight and responsibility of making things work on my own.

> *"If you can believe,*
> *all things are possible to him*
> *who believes."*
> Mark 9:23 (NKJV)

About two months later I met James, my husband and the love of my life, in the most unexpected way: through an internet dating site. I had always said that I would not find love that way, and in fact, I had never accepted a date from a dating site before James, but God has a sense of humor! Looking back, this was a great example of how God truly will use anything to fulfill His will. It even seems sometimes like He uses the things we least expect to bring about what we desire the most, just to put His undisputed fingerprint on it!

    I didn't think or believe internet dating was a romantic way to meet my true love. As a birthday gift, my friends bought me a one-year membership to a dating site, and when I refused to create a profile, they created one for me! Even then, I didn't really use it or try to pursue anyone. This was mostly because I didn't find anyone that caught my attention, and I wasn't attracted to the guys that tried to pursue me. When my subscription expired, I gave a negative review on the survey, advising that the site didn't work to bring me even a single match. As a result, the site extended my membership for three more months. Shortly after, James Collins "winked" at me on the site. For once, the guy trying to get my attention was really cute! Intrigued, I read his profile and found him to also be an interesting person.

    I "winked" back at him, which was so weird to me, but I'm glad I got over the awkwardness of it all. We started up a conversation, exchanging messages for a couple of weeks before he invited me to meet in person.

THE JOY OF BECOMING

I arrived before him on our first date, and I remember being nervous while waiting for him. However, when he walked into that bar smiling and immediately gave me a warm hug, I felt comfortable and at peace with him. We started talking and we had so much in common. The connection between us was instant and strong!

Now, when I look back, I know that moment when we hugged for the first time was the moment; I knew he was the one! Crazy, right? We talked a lot that night. It was a Friday night, and we enjoyed each other's company so much that we went out again the next day. Then again, the day after that! It happened to be Super Bowl Sunday, and we met after the Super Bowl to catch a movie. In all, we had five dates in the first eight days after meeting each other in person. We haven't been apart since.

Everything happened very quickly, but every step of our relationship happened the way I always dreamed it would happen! From the way he honored me and asked for my parents' blessing to marry me, to his amazingly romantic proposal, to our two wedding ceremonies, the way he loves and respects me daily, and how he believes in me and pushes me to be my best! I could not have dreamed of a better match than the one God had prepared for me!

It has been an amazing journey so far! Of course, we have faced mountains and valleys together, learning and growing through struggles, but we choose to love and respect each other every single day. My devotion to James and our family grows more and more every day, and I choose us forever!

What I want you to get out of my story is that the desires God has put on your heart are yours. He knows every little detail of what you want, and your desires are not insignificant to him. He will deliver accordingly, at precisely the right time, when you are aligned with Him and His will for your life.

What do you really want for your life? Surrender it all to God! Surrender the things that no longer serve you, forgive yourself and others for what needs to be forgiven, and let go of anything that is holding you back. Believe and expect God's plans for your life are both good and possible. God is always working all things together for your good!

THE JOY OF BECOMING

Your future depends on you saying "yes" and stepping out in faith in what God is calling you to. When you make a choice to design the life you want to live and ask God to guide you on the path He has for you, everything starts shifting in your favor!

> *"Therefore, I tell you, whatever you ask for in prayer, believe that you have received it, and it will be yours."*
>
> Mark 11:24 (NIV)

You have been given one chance to live this life, and you don't know when you will take your last breath, so make the best of every minute you have and enjoy the gift of life!

When you envision your dream life, let go of your limiting beliefs and judgmental thoughts; just dream! Visualize, journal, feel all the feelings of living that life, and ask God to reveal to you His plans for your future.

Cast a Vision

Most importantly, imagine the person you need to be to live your dream life. Understanding how you think, feel and behave while living that life will enable the necessary transformation and breakthroughs to take place for you to become the person you need to be to receive and experience the amazing life God has for you. Everything God takes us through in life is meant to teach us and help us grow into the person He needs us to be. His favor and blessing flow through our faith in Him and our obedience to following His direction. Your personal growth will take place as you begin to learn who you are now, your strengths and weaknesses, and understand the gap between who you are now and the person you are destined to become.

That night in my room when I cried out to God, He took away the weight and the pressure I was carrying in the process of trying to find my future husband on my own. Let my experience be a lesson for you. You don't have to do things on your own strength either. Before we move forward, if you've never done so before, I want to give you the opportunity to invite Jesus into your life. Even if you have invited him into your life before, just take the opportunity to reinforce your commitment to living for Christ. He will meet you right where you are now.

Lay it all down at the feet of Jesus, any burdens, weight, pressure, sadness, depression, anxiety, discouragement, disappointment, or desire for control. Let go of whatever you are carrying on your own that is heavy or is no longer serving you and let Him take it from you.

Now, pray this prayer with me:

"Dear Jesus, thank you for your sacrifice in dying on the cross to save me. I repent from my sins, and I ask for forgiveness. Please come into my heart and be the Lord of my life. Take control of my life and make it a living testimony to your glory. Help me to be more like you, by the power of the Holy Spirit, so I can live the life You died to give me. In your name, I pray. Amen."

Congratulations! This is the first step toward the most amazing life transformation and freedom you can ever experience in your life.

I'm so happy and excited for you, beautiful!

Time for Reflection:

1. What does your dream life look like?

2. What kind of person do you need to be to live that life?

2. Be Specific

It is possible to miss-live your life. I don't know about you, but I remember a time when I felt like I had no control over my life. I was just going with the flow and not being intentional or even knowing what my next steps were. It was not very fun. I remember being frustrated, negative and complaining a lot. I could not find the good in anything because I was focusing on the bad and feeling sorry for myself while blaming everything, and everyone, around me for the way I was feeling. I isolated myself and didn't want to be around other people. I didn't even want to be around myself, but I just wouldn't go away!

I found myself lacking direction and wasting time focusing on the wrong things. That was because I allowed life to take over. I was just reacting to whatever life threw at me. It might sound easy to live by default and just go with it, but there is no way to experience fulfillment that way. You end up chasing an elusive "something" that you can't even put your finger on, so you stay in a constant state of wanting. I had to decide

Be Specific

to take responsibility and control of my life and start making the changes I needed to design the life I wanted to live. But first, I had to clarify what kind of life I wanted to live.

After nearly four years of marriage and welcoming our first child, Zoey, to the world, James was offered an incredible job opportunity that would require us to move from San Diego to Dallas. My growth in starting to understand the importance of living a life by design began after we made this move in December 2017. It was an extremely hard transition for me. Even though we were praying for the blessing we would receive here, like a bigger house, the opportunity for me to stay home with Zoey and grow our family, financial blessings, and new opportunities for James in his career, I didn't want to let go of the life I had in beautiful San Diego.

My husband was born and raised in Texas, so since we got married, he had the desire to come back to Dallas and stay close to his family. I didn't. I loved San Diego, and we had a good life there. I used to tell him, "In order for me to move to TX, God would need to work out the best opportunity, so there would be no way I could say no to it".

Well, be careful what you pray for and ask others to stand in agreement with, as the Bible says.

> *"Again, I say to you that if two of you agree on earth concerning anything that they ask, it will be done for them by My Father in heaven."*
>
> Matthew 18:19

In 2017, James received a promotion at his job in San Diego, and we were so excited about it. We had been praying for a couple of years for this promotion, as we thought it would be the answer to everything we were hoping for. However, when we learned all the details of it, it was not even close to what we were expecting and believing in. As a result, we were disappointed and discouraged, not knowing God's plans or being able to see the big picture.

Be Specific

Shortly after that, James got a call from an old friend from Texas. They had worked together two different times before, at two different companies. He was calling to tell James about a job opportunity he had available, and he thought James would be a great fit for it.

Long story short, when God's timing hits, things move fast! The conversation started in September 2017 and after some time interviewing and negotiating his offer, on December 13, 2017, we moved to Frisco Texas. We didn't even need to lift a finger. The company James was going to work for packed and shipped all our belongings, including our cars, and gave us a substantial sum of money in cash to make the move. The amazing opportunity I said God needed to present to us for me to move to Texas was right in front of us. Even though I didn't want to move, I could not bring myself to say "no" to a great opportunity.

The next few months were crazy, exciting, and sad, a mix of many emotions, while having to make big decisions about jobs, selling our house, moving to a different state, finding a new church and so many more decisions. We found out we were pregnant not long before our move, and I experienced a miscarriage in that same period. We also had to say "goodbye" to my sister who had been living with us for the last 6 months, and my parents that were visiting as well. Then, boom! Within a blink of an eye, we were on a plane flying to Dallas while our cars and belongings were being transported by truck.

The next thing I knew, I was a stay-at-home mom. One of the big decisions I had to make was to let go of my career to focus on my family. My husband and I agreed that was the best decision for our family at the time. I had the opportunity to be a full-time mom for Zoey, and later welcome Noah to complete our family. I love being a mother, it's my favorite role, but it is also a 24-hour job with very different compensation! This was something I had to take time to get used to. If you are a mother, you probably understand exactly what I'm trying to say here.

During this season, I also felt lost, lonely, and tired, like I was not using my full potential. I started comparing myself with other women who all seemed to have it figured out, while I most certainly did not. I had an amazing life, an amazing husband, great kids,

Be Specific

friends, a fabulous church community, and a beautiful home. I was experiencing the life I prayed for! However, I felt like there was something missing inside of me. I couldn't help but feel like there was more in life than what I was experiencing, and I was not living out my calling or living up to my full potential.

But God had a plan, as He always does. He was working in me and through me. There was a transformation in progress. I felt like I had lost so much in the transition from California to Texas. Because I didn't take the time to process and mourn then, I was not able to let go of the thoughts, beliefs, and things I needed to in order to see and receive all the blessings God was giving me. The verse God showed me in that season was:

> *"Be still and know that I am God."*
> Psalm 46:10

As I leaned closer to God and asked for help, expecting Him to guide me, I began to hear Him speaking to me more and more clearly. He challenged me to just stay still. It was very hard for me to obey this guidance, but I knew I had to do it. After all, I had said "yes" to His plans in moving us to Texas, and I knew deep inside that God had a great plan for me and my family. Therefore, I focused on what was important in that season for my family and for myself. I took the time to think about and clarify what mattered the most to me like my family, my faith and relationship with God, other key relationships in my life, where I experienced fulfillment, and the legacy I wanted to leave. I had to invest in my relationship with God, allow myself to take the time to process my emotions, and allow God to guide me and heal me.

The transformation took time, it was over a year before I was able to process it all and be able to change my perspective about our move to Texas. I went from thinking about all that I felt I had lost when I moved to Texas, to considering how God was moving certain things out of my life, things that no longer served me or were holding me back from moving towards what He had next for me so that I could progress to what He had in store for me next.

Now I understand how much I needed to change and transform myself from the inside out to be able to receive it and step out in faith to where God was calling

Be Specific

me. My heart needed to be healed, and my mind needed to be in the right place.

> *"And we know that in all things God works for the good of those who love him, who have been called according to his purpose.*
>
> Romans 8:28 (NIV)

God also showed me I needed to be grateful for all that I had, that I needed to be present in the moment, to find joy in each season of my life, to look for goodness in everyday life, and to choose joy.

I want you to see, hear, and feel in my story that all things are possible, and you can achieve whatever you want for your life if you are willing to pay the price. The price will be different for each person, but you can rest assured it will likely be something hard you will need to overcome. I will be honest with you; it won't be easy. But you will reap a harvest if you are willing to do the work!

THE JOY OF BECOMING

Keep your eyes on God and His promises, on His strength, not yours. Be bold and keep pushing yourself, and you will break off the things holding you back from living the life God intended for you to live.

Being specific about your vision will allow you to eliminate distractions and establish the right disciplines to create the reality you choose. Remember that an opportunity is not a good opportunity if it is not aligned with your vision or is not moving you closer to the life you want to live. A meaningful and detailed vision will bring you excitement and joy every day. It will be a constant motivator for you, even on really hard days. *Especially* on really hard days!

Now, it's time to dream about the specifics. What exactly does your best life look like? You need to dig into the details. Thinking about the specifics will help you imagine and feel like your dream can become your reality. Having a clear vision of what you want will inspire and motivate you to keep moving toward it.

www.themariacollins.com

Time for Reflection: Consider the following questions as they pertain to your "ideal life" to help you be specific with what you want:

1. Where do you live?

2. Who are the people in your life?

3. What material things do you have? (e.g.: house, car, vacation properties, etc.)

4. What's your day like? Do you work, have a business, or raise a family full-time?

3. Find What Matters Most

Life has different seasons, and as you navigate the different seasons of your life, your priorities and focus might change. But when you know the things that matter the most to you, you can design a rhythm for each season and create a balance between the things you want to accomplish and making time for what matters most to you.

After I became a mom, my world turned upside-down. Everything changed. At first, I thought I could do it all: work full-time, have a great career, and be the best mom and wife. But I was overwhelmed, stressed, and I felt guilty every day when I left my baby girl at daycare. It was a constant battle in my head and heart.

Life was not what I expected after having my baby girl. I didn't understand how other women were able to do it all and have multiple kids. Here I was struggling to manage it all with just one kid. I remember thinking "that's it". I won't be able to do anything else other than be a mom. Everything else is over.

Find What Matters Most

Now I see that I was overwhelmed with all the changes happening so fast. I was afraid of losing myself on top of dealing with hormones and emotions. I was trying to figure out a new dynamic for our family while wanting to be back to my old body. At the time, I needed to be reminded of what the bible says about seasons, and just focus on what was important at that time.

> *"There is a time for everything, and a season for every activity under the heavens"*
> Ecclesiastes 3:1 (NIV)

However, I didn't know how to stay in the moment and enjoy the process of growing and learning to be a mom. I wanted to accomplish it all right then. I was focusing on the future and the things I wanted to do, like going back to work. The job I had at the time was a job I truly enjoyed. It was my first corporate job in America since I left Brazil about 10 years prior, and I was building confidence in my abilities as a business leader. Every struggle I felt as a new mother was a reminder of how much I missed being a professional.

THE JOY OF BECOMING

I remember the breastfeeding process being particularly challenging when I had to sit for long periods of time to feed my baby girl or pump. I saw it all as frustrating, hard, and painful, instead of a blessing to be able to take that time to feed my precious baby girl and to nurse my ailing body back to a new normal. I know now my thoughts and mindset were not fixed on the right things. I say that because when I welcomed Noah, my second baby, three years later, my experience with breastfeeding was completely different, because my mind and thoughts were improved.

God is good all the time, and all the time God is good! He is a great father! He is always working all things together for your good and his glory. He also gives you free will to make decisions and go the way you want in life. From my experience, now I understand that in every season, and every next level of blessings, there is a need for me to grow and stretch myself into the person prepared to receive those blessings. At the same time, I need to show God I'm a good steward of what He has already blessed me with if I expect Him to trust me with more.

Find What Matters Most

It took Moses forty years to lead the children of Israel to the promised land; a distance they could have traversed in eleven days. Why is that? When I was reading that story recently, I saw how ungrateful, negative, and unfaithful the people were. All they did was complain and forget every miracle God did along the way. "We are just going to die here" they would say, and many did. But that's not how the story had to go for them. It is certainly not the way God would have preferred it to go. He was clearly frustrated with His children's lack of faithfulness and obedience in the face of so many visible miracles that their God was with them and for them.

Because they could not be grateful, learn, trust, grow and show stewardship for all that God was doing for them through Moses, it took them more than 1,328 times as long to reach the promised land as it should have. What areas of your own life are you delaying God's promises for you through disobedience, lack of faith, poor stewardship, and complaining instead of praising Him for everything He's already done?

For me, the transition into motherhood was a struggle, and I believe it had to do with the fact that I was not taking time to enjoy the process or appreciate the opportunity to slow down. I have always been very active and did not walk into that season with the right focus and mindset. If any of this resonates with you and the season of life you are in now, I want you to know that God is for you, he loves you, and his plans for you are good. If you feel lost or you don't really know what matters the most to you, you can just ask God to reveal to you what that is, or what it should be. Ask him to change your heart and mind and fill you with the Holy Spirit to guide you.

Confess, surrender, and repent of the things that you have in your life now that are not aligned with God's way and don't serve you. You can always turn to God and ask for help. That is what he wants; for you to lean on him and use his ways because they are better than your ways. It took me a while to learn that, and I still remind myself of that often. I hope this serves you and benefits you in your own life.

Time for Reflection: Consider the following questions as they pertain to what matters the most to you:

1. What matters the most to you?

2. List the people that are most important to you and the reason why.

4. Establish Core Values

Core values are the fundamental principles and characteristics that influence your behavior and impact every decision you make. In short, your core values signal to the world who you *choose* to be, in every moment and in every situation. One of the most empowering truths about life is that we have been given the power to choose much of what we experience. This all starts with choosing who we will be, regardless of what we see around us. Understanding your core values and what you judge as most important about who you are will guide you to live a life based on what matters the most, a purposeful life.

Whether you are aware of it or not, you are living by certain core values. Most people live by unconscious values and never get clear on what they value most or why. If you live life this way, you will be a product of your circumstances rather than staying true to yourself no matter what life throws at you. If you take time to purposefully clarify and define your core values, you can start to live intentionally, and *you* get to dictate what your life will be about instead of allowing circumstances to dictate this for you. Your behavior and decision-making will not depend on what happens around you but will be based on your values and consequently on whom you choose to be.

Did you know that the average person makes more than 35,000 decisions a day? That seems like a lot of decisions to me. If you take out eight hours for sleeping, it comes out to an average of 2,187 decisions per hour, or 36 decisions per minute. Most of those decisions are completely unconscious. We aren't mindful of every one of these decisions, because most of the decisions we make are automatic. This is where your core values are put into action! Your beliefs, experiences, and environment have trained you to live a certain way and dictate most of these automatic decisions for you. When you get clear about your core values, you can retrain your brain to make automatic decisions that align with your values so that who you *say* you are is consistent with who you *actually* are in your decisions and behavior.

THE JOY OF BECOMING

If you are done feeling like there is more in life than what you are currently experiencing, I invite you to take the time to define the top five core values you want to live by. It is possible for you to consistently be the person you want to be if you have a clear vision of who that is, what that version of yourself values, and be intentional and focused, taking one step at a time, one decision at a time to be that person. You won't always make the right decisions, and you won't always act the way the best version of yourself should act. That's where grace comes in. However, with time and practice, you'll see that you naturally act and react in ways that align with your ideal self, more often than not.

If you don't know or have never thought about your core values, let me help you discover your own top five core values. Below is a list of examples of personal values to help you. Read through it and highlight the ones that resonate with you. Then, read the highlighted ones and narrow them down to the five values that are most important to you. Feel free to add any other values that come to mind that are not part of the list.

Establish Core Values

Accomplishment	Gratitude	Purpose
Achievement	Greatness	Recognition
Accountability	Growth	Regularity
Accuracy	Happiness	Relationships
Adventure	Hard work	Reliability
Attitude	Harmony	Resourcefulness
Beauty	Health	Respect
Calm	Honesty	Responsibility
Challenge	Improvement	Results-oriented
Change	Independence	Security
Collaboration	Individuality	Self-giving
Commitment	Innovation	Self-reliance
Communication	Integrity	Self-thinking
Community	Intuitiveness	Service
Comfort	Justice	Simplicity
Compassion	Joy	Skill
Competence	Knowledge	Problem solver
Competition	Leadership	Speed
Connection	Learning	Spontaneity
Cooperation	Love	Standardization
Coordination	Loyalty	Status
Creativity	Management	Safety
Decisiveness	Meaning	Satisfaction
Delight	Modeling	Stewardship
Democracy	Money	Strong-willed
Discipline	Openness	Structure
Discovery	Orderliness	Success
Diversity	Passion	Teamwork

THE JOY OF BECOMING

Efficiency	Peace	Techniques
Empowerment	Perfection	Timeliness
Excellence	Personal Choice	Tolerance
Fairness	Pleasure	Tradition
Faith	Power	Transformation
Family	Positivity	Tranquility
Flair	Practicality	Trust
Flexibility	Preservation	Truth
Focus	Privacy	Unity
Freedom	Productive	Variety
Friendship	Progress	Wealth
Fun	Prosperity	Wellness
Good health	Punctuality	Wisdom

After you have picked your top five, list them below:

1. _____
2. _____
3. _____
4. _____
5. _____

I'm so excited for you! Helping others establish their core values is one of my favorite things to do as a coach, as I experienced a transformation in my life after establishing and deciding to live by my core values. The decision-making process in my mind became so much faster and easier. No matter what I face, my

Establish Core Values

decisions are based on my personal core values which are:

Excellence: I always give my best in anything and everything I do.

Faith (relationship with God): God is at the center of my life, and I invest time in growing my relationship with Him every day.

Family (relationship with husband and kids): they are my favorite people, and I want to have the best relationship and live the best life by their side.

Gratitude: an attitude of gratitude has the power to change my perspective in any circumstance.

Balance: I intentionally spend the right amount of time on the things that I value most; myself, my family, my career, fun, and rest.

When I'm coaching a client in identifying her core values, I advise her to take a week and spend time every day evaluating her thoughts and actions to bring awareness to how her decision-making is programmed. I ask her to observe herself for a week, paying close attention to every decision she makes and the forces influencing those decisions. You can practice this yourself. Take notes and journal your experience during the week.

Which automatic decisions are in line with who you most want to be? Think about why that is and write about the connection you feel to those decisions. For instance, did you wake up and decide to pray first thing in the morning, or go to the gym for a workout? Did these actions tap into your desire to put your spiritual and physical health above all else? There are core values at the heart of those desires.

> *"The hearts of the wise make their mouths prudent, and their lips promote instruction"*
> Proverbs 16:23 (NIV)

Also, think about the decisions you made that did not align with who you most want to be. For instance, maybe you decided to cheat on your diet and have sweets late at night. Perhaps that speaks to a

Establish Core Values

level of discipline that is lacking in you and that needs to be strengthened for you to reach your true potential.

Practicing this level of mindfulness will teach you so much about yourself and make you aware of what is influencing you or potentially holding you back. You can then decide to eliminate what does not serve you or does not fit in with the lifestyle you want to live and start making all your decisions based on the values you truly want to live by. If this is something new to you, I want to help you make the transformation process easy and more enjoyable. Remember to have fun and love yourself in the process!

Write your core values down and make them visible to you. Every morning read them out loud to yourself and make the decision to live by your core values. First, you might need to remind yourself multiple times a day, which is part of the process. So, trust the process and keep going, and be consistent with it. Pretty soon you will have them memorized, and you will be able to recall them in the moment as you are making decisions. The more times you make a conscious decision to live by your values, the more you train your brain to make similar decisions unconsciously. Eventually, this leads to a life lived consistently with what you value most at the heart of everything you do!

Every day repeat to yourself, "every decision I make will be based on my core values. No circumstances, people, or anything out of my control will affect my decision." Then read aloud your top five core values. You may even decide to create declarations for each of your core values. I highly recommend this to cement your values with the driving motivation behind them. For instance, one of my personal daily declarations is, "I plan effectively and stick to my plan so that I always have proper *balance* in the things that matter most to me." Continue to journal and track your progress and celebrate little wins along the way. Remember, whatever you feed in life will grow, whatever you starve will die! You got this girl!

www.themariacollins.com

Time for Reflection:

1. List your 5 core values and what each one means to you.

5. Know Your "Why"

Your "why" is the reason you do anything and everything in life. It's what motivates and excites you to keep moving, even when you don't feel like it. Knowing and connecting strongly to your "why" will enable you to build disciplines that serve your higher purpose, endure hardships along your path and persevere when others would give up. Friedrich Nietzsche once said, "He who has a "why" to live for can bear almost any how." In other words, if you have a clear purpose for what you're doing, even the hard things that must be done to accomplish it will be worth doing!

At the beginning of this book, I wrote about the importance of casting a vision for your life. Your "why" is the driving force behind your vision, because it gives your vision purpose. Think about the importance of a vision statement for a company. It sets the direction and becomes the "why" behind everything that the company sets out to do. The same is true for your life. The Bible says that having a long-term vision in life is so important that we die without it!

Know Your "WHY"

> *"Where there is no vision, the people perish"*
>
> Proverbs 29:18 (KJV)

The reason I do everything I do is to bring God's light into this world and to build a legacy that will glorify God for generations. I strive to teach my kids, my clients, and anyone else I am privileged to influence to take possession of the promises God has for them, to live with purpose, and to glorify God by being good stewards of the gifts and talents He has given them. I pray every day for God to use me as His vessel to touch the lives of others in a loving, positive, and motivational way to help them see their value, to empower them to go after what they want, and to live the life God intends for them to live.

I want everything in life that God has prepared for me, including amazing relationships with my husband, kids, extended family, and friends. I want an abundant life with plenty of the good things in life: prosperity, joy, and fulfillment. I want success in my business and to make an impact as an author, coach, and speaker, but I also want to control my time and use it wisely to experience balance in life. I want financial freedom, to create wealth, and to build a legacy that will last for generations. I'm extremely grateful to be experiencing so many things in my life that once were only dreams and prayers.

Like everyone else, I'm a work in progress. I love to learn, grow, and become better than I was yesterday as I strive to be more like Jesus. I want to lead by example, be an energy producer and show other women that nothing is impossible with God. God has been working in me and through me to transform my body, spirit, and soul to become the person He needs me to be to do the work He planned for me.

However, I haven't always been as dedicated to pursuing my purpose as I am today. During some seasons of life, I felt lost, lacked direction, felt discontented, frustrated, less than, unfulfilled, and generally like there was more in life than what I was experiencing. Now as I look back, I see that I needed to grow, stretch myself, learn, and have the confidence to step to the next level. This required me to revise my focus, understand my desires, and make sure it was all aligned with God and my core values. Most importantly, I had to go back to my "why", the reason I do anything and everything in my life.

Knowing what you want and understanding the reasons why you want to achieve anything in life will strengthen you in hard times when you feel discouraged, and things get in your way.

> *"Let us not become weary in doing good, for at the proper time we will reap a harvest if we do not give up."*
> Galatians 6:9 (NIV)

There will always be something in your way. The enemy of your soul does not want you to succeed, and he works hard to leverage your weaknesses to get in your way, isolate you and make you think you are not enough.

> *"Be sober, be vigilant;*
> *because your adversary the devil*
> *walks about like a roaring lion,*
> *seeking whom he may devour"*
>
> 1 Peter 5:8 (NKJV)

By knowing your "why" and having God by your side, you will be more likely to act when you don't feel like it, pick yourself up when you fall, and stay on the path.

Now it is your turn to write down your "why." Stop and take time to reflect and ask God to reveal to you the things you should prioritize. What gets you fired up and sparks passion in you? In what ways do you want to make your life more than just about you? Take three deep breaths, clear your mind and just write down what comes to you without any judgment.

Time for Reflection: Consider the following questions as they relate to your "WHY" to help you be specific with what that means to you:

1. What is your "WHY?"

2. What fires you up and sparks passion in you?

3. Which ways would you like to make your life more than just about you?

PART II

Assessing

The Life You Have

6. Take Inventory

Once you've set a clear vision for your life, grounded yourself in your core values, and discovered the "why" behind how you choose to spend your life, it's time to take inventory of your life to identify how you are, or aren't, making progress toward your purpose. Taking inventory is an essential practice for business accounting to have a complete list of stock, materials, office supplies and anything else that is required to turn a profit. The same practice can help you better understand what is or isn't working in your life to support your mission.

Taking inventory of your life will help you understand where your time and energy are going so you can be more intentional about how you live and better support yourself in fulfilling your dreams. Especially if you feel stuck or in a rut in life, taking inventory can help identify habits, time wasters, and mission killers that might be contributing to how you are feeling. This could make all the difference between you living life by default versus living life by design.

THE JOY OF BECOMING

Understanding everything that currently comprises your life will help you see what needs to stay and what needs to go. Taking inventory is a practice I regularly engage in to ensure the things I do or have in my life are aligned with my values and the way I want to live. Anything that does not match my vision for the life I want to live must be purposefully eliminated.

Awareness is the first step to bringing about meaningful change in your life. You can't change anything if you aren't aware that it needs to be changed. Only by slowing down to acknowledge how you are living your life can you make the decision to change or eliminate what doesn't serve you. When you take inventory, it helps you to break the big picture down to its various components so you can recognize the things or people that are not aligned with the person you want to be, or the life you want to live. You will be empowered to remove whatever you want from your life and open space for new things and new people that are in alignment with what you want in your environment.

When I'm coaching a woman to take inventory of her life, I ask her to start by analyzing a week of her

Take Inventory

life. This starts by journaling your days. Take note of everything you do from the time you wake up to the time you fall asleep and pay attention to how you feel about what you do every hour of your day. This practice will help you see everything you are spending your energy and time on currently. While doing this, it is important to pay attention to your emotions. Your emotions are signing your body gives you, a message that something might not be right. Allow yourself to feel it and explore where it is coming from by thinking about what triggered the emotion, to begin with. Did something out of your control happen? What were you thinking or doing when the emotion started?

After a week of intentionally tracking where your time goes, you will be amazed at how the practice helps you see things you do without even noticing, especially the things you do even though they serve no real purpose for you, or habits you currently have that are not supporting the life you want to live. Whatever you have been doing to get to where you are in life will not take you to the next level. To level up your life, you must level up your habits. If you can't see what needs to be changed, stopped, surrendered, or forgiven, you can't do anything about it.

THE JOY OF BECOMING

I want to invite you to do this practice yourself for a week. It will open your eyes to see your reality and identify the gap between where you are and where you want to be. It will also support you in your next steps of intentionally designing the best rhythm for your life.

> *"The one who gets wisdom loves life; the one who cherishes understanding will soon prosper."*
> Proverbs 19:8 (NIV)

God intends for you to live an amazing life. His plans are to give you hope and a future; not to harm you but to love you, support you, and give you strength through any season. To take a step forward, ask God to reveal to you anything you are not seeing that need to change, areas of darkness that needs to be brought to light, or sins you need to repent from and ask Him to change your heart and fill you with the Holy Spirit. Don't be afraid. God is an amazing father. He meets you exactly where you are and loves you through the process, exactly the way you need to be guided and loved.

Take Inventory

While you are registering all you do, please don't be hard on yourself or pass judgment. Remember you are doing this to grow and become a better version of yourself. That requires you to investigate things that don't make you feel good about yourself, or that you know you should not be doing. It takes courage to do what you need to do here, girl, and I want to say I'm proud of you and I can't wait for you to experience all the freedom and empowerment that comes from deciding to make necessary changes and take control of your life! I also suggest finding a close friend, or your spouse, and confessing the things that have been holding you back, and the lies the enemy has been using against you to keep you stuck in darkness.

> *"Therefore, confess your sins to each other and pray for each other so that you may be healed. The prayer of a righteous person is powerful and effective."*
> James 5:16 (NIV

THE JOY OF BECOMING

As women, we tend to be hard on ourselves. Please notice if you start moving in this direction. catch your thoughts, feelings, and self-talk, and hold it all captive to make it loving and supportive to yourself. Remember what the Bible says:

> *"We demolish arguments and every pretension that sets itself up against the knowledge of God, and we take captive every thought to make it obedient to Christ."*
>
> 2 Corinthians 10:5 (NIV)

Now that your eyes are open to see the things, thoughts, habits, or people you no longer need in your life, it is time to do something about it. Are you ready to make some changes?

After you have journaled about the things you do daily, review them and highlight what no longer serves you or is no longer aligned with the person you want to become.

Take Inventory

Next, make a list of tasks, habits, thoughts, beliefs, and activities you want to implement into your life that will help you grow into the person you want to be. For example, if your goal is to lose weight, you need to prioritize and focus your thoughts on your health. Plan and prepare meals and snacks for your week and start moving your body. If your goal is to grow your relationship with God, you need to spend time reading His word, praying, worshiping, seeking Him, and falling in love with Him.

Start substituting the habits you don't want with the new habits you need to implement in your life. Be consistent and find an accountability partner to help you stay on track. You can do this, girl! I believe in you!

Now that you have taken inventory of where your energy goes and how you spend your time daily, I want you to evaluate different areas of your life. This will also give you a better understanding of your reality and help you identify areas in your life that can be re-engineered to foster more joy, excitement, and fulfillment in your life! The faster you acknowledge and take responsibility for the way you are living now, the faster you can adjust to achieve what you want. If you continue to do what you have been doing, you will continue to get what you have been getting out of life. If you want a different outcome, you will need to use a different approach.

If I asked you to rate your life right now on how satisfied you are on a scale of 1 to 10, what number would you pick? Be honest with yourself. Go ahead, say it out loud and hear the truth of how you feel about your life. It is ok, remember awareness is the first step toward any transformation. Don't be afraid to face the truth of how you really feel.

No matter what number you pick, life can always get better. And if the way you are living your life right now is not what you want for your future, you are on the right path. This book found its way to you for a reason, so allow it to transform and improve your life. You are looking for ways to grow and change for the better, and I'm so proud of you! Do not miss your breakthrough by reading this but refuse to do the work you need to do in yourself to change!

So far, you have dreamed about your best life, listed the things that matter the most to you, established your core values, identified and clarified

Take Inventory

your "why," and taken inventory of your life. At this point in my coaching program, my clients have more clarity about the kind of life they want, and they have grown in their awareness of the things that need to be changed. This next step will help you create a clear picture of how well your current habits are serving you in key areas of your life. Perform an honest evaluation of each area below on a scale of 1 to 10 (1 = worst situation and 10 = best situation)

Life Awareness Exercise

Self-care	1	2	3	4	5	6	7	8	9	10
Health	1	2	3	4	5	6	7	8	9	10
Joy	1	2	3	4	5	6	7	8	9	10
Romantic Relationship	1	2	3	4	5	6	7	8	9	10
Family	1	2	3	4	5	6	7	8	9	10
Friendship	1	2	3	4	5	6	7	8	9	10
Career	1	2	3	4	5	6	7	8	9	10
Finances	1	2	3	4	5	6	7	8	9	10
Spirituality	1	2	3	4	5	6	7	8	9	10
Fun	1	2	3	4	5	6	7	8	9	10
Consistency	1	2	3	4	5	6	7	8	9	10

TOTAL _____

Having completed this assessment, you should start to get a clear picture of what areas of your life need the most attention. Which areas did you rate the lowest? What might be contributing to your rating of those areas? What is causing you to feel this way? Look for the root cause of the matter. What is lacking, missing, or needed that is under your control to

Take Inventory

improve those specific areas? This practice enables you to see the discrepancy between where you are now and where you would like to be. By bringing mindful awareness to this, you can begin to be more intentional and identify successful strategies and implement long-lasting habits to achieve and sustain a higher level of success in those areas of your life.

As women, we tend to underestimate our accomplishments. Most of us do not know how to celebrate the little wins and successes accomplished every day. It is only by stacking little wins consistently over time that we can experience the big wins we all dream about.

I'm guilty of it, and I'm still learning to celebrate my wins no matter how big or small. When you are constantly focusing on what is next, you don't take the time to celebrate the little accomplishments at the moment and appreciate the growth journey you are on. If you can't celebrate the little wins along the way, you won't fully appreciate the big wins when you achieve them as well. Remember this: until your days on earth are through, there is no final destination, only new mountains to climb. Learn to find joy in the journey!

THE JOY OF BECOMING

To this end, it is helpful to recall your past successes. Perhaps you have had more accomplishments than what you give yourself credit for. I say that because I have been there, but I've learned to be more intentional about giving myself credit for my hard work. I still have room for improvement, but I'm getting better every day and so can you! What I learned is that it all comes down to being intentional and making time for what matters to me. Celebrating my accomplishments and the accomplishments of those I love matters.

If you have a hard time recognizing your accomplishments, or you feel like you have not achieved much lately, I want to invite you to make a list of all that you have accomplished in the last ten years. Consider where you were ten years ago and start listing everything you've accomplished between then and now. Try to be specific and look for little wins in addition to the big ones. Maybe you paid off a credit card, learned a new skill, or found love. Perhaps you bought your first house or gave birth to a child (or three). Whatever it is, taking time to reflect on your life will help you identify and celebrate the times you have found victory in life, and this will help you increase your

Take Inventory

belief that victory is achievable at higher levels in your future.

I did this exercise myself in 2020, recalling all my accomplishments since 2010. Year by year, month by month as I thought about and wrote down my list, I felt so proud of myself. I was able to see God's hand in my life all the way, orchestrating every step of the journey. So many things happened, and I experienced so many changes in my life in those years that I had completely forgotten about or taken for granted. However, performing this exercise allowed me to bring back those memories. It felt amazing, and I was so grateful!

The timing was perfect for me, as 2020 was exactly ten years since I moved to the United States. In 2010 I moved to San Diego, California to participate in an exchange program to be an Au Pair, improve my English, and experience and learn a different culture. This decision absolutely transformed my future! I completed my master's degree in San Diego, I met my husband and got married there, and we bought our first house and had our first child together there. San Diego is also where I had my first corporate leadership role where I got to put my education and talent to use as a consultant for law firms. This time period also included our move to Texas, finding our church and family of choice here, having our son, and the beginning of my exploration into God's calling on my life as an entrepreneur, coach, and consultant for other female entrepreneurs.

In 2020, God knew I needed a reminder of all that I had accomplished and assurance that He was with me every step of the way. He was the one who opened all the doors and gave me the courage to walk through them. That was the reminder I needed that all things are possible with Him and that He was ready to do more of his wonderful works! I just needed to trust Him and move in faith.

I don't know what you might be experiencing right now, but I want to remind you that no matter what, God is for you, and nothing is impossible with Him. Take the time to review the last ten years of your life. Consider all of your accomplishments. Think about how all of those accomplishments came about and find the miracles of God along the way. Whatever He did once he can do again. Trust in Him, get out of the way,

Take Inventory

surrender control, and be ready to move when He tells you to.

www.themariacollins.com

Time for Reflection: Consider the following practices to assist you to take inventory:

1. How are you using your time? Journal every hour of your day for a week. Then revise and eliminate what no longer serves you.

2. Journal your last 10 years' accomplishments? You are going to be amazed at how far you have come.

Get your **FREE BONUS RESOURCES** at:
www.TheMariaCollins.com

Download the Fast Action Workbook that accompanies this book to help you clarify your vision, experience freedom, and live with Passion, Purpose, and Prosperity.

The Fast Action Guide includes:
The 7 days daily hour tracker journal
The 10 years accomplishment journal and more

7. Navigating Every Season

Every year we experience four different seasons where the weather, nature, the position of the earth, human routine, and behavior all change. There is Spring, Summer, Autumn, and Winter, and each one presents its own distinct weather patterns and unique daylight hours caused by the earth's moving position relative to the sun.

According to each season, our eating, sleeping, and dress patterns change to adjust appropriately to its characteristics. During the winter it is cold, with shorter days, and longer nights. Most people tend to eat and drink what keeps them warm. They tend to stay inside and warm with fire and blankets, dress up cozy and wear lots of layers. In the summer when it is hot, the opposite happens with most people wanting refreshing drinks and food, spending more time outdoors, playing with water, and wearing light clothing to stay cool.

Winter and summer are the extreme seasons, where everything is very different, but we also have the transitional seasons of spring and autumn when the changes happen slowly right in front of us, and we get to watch the transformation of nature. During spring, which succeeds winter when mainly vegetation goes dormant, the seeds take root, all vegetation sprouts again, the colors return, and the animals and humans become more active. There is a feeling of new beginnings and revival. Autumn is a very active and fun season where most people enjoy the weather outside, kids are in school, and we prepare for the end-of-year holidays. When fall comes the weather starts to cool down, daylight shortens, and leaves change colors and begin to fall. It is a season to slow down, get cozy, and prepare for winter.

Consider the four seasons as they relate to farming activities. I'm not an expert, but from what I have observed, spring is the time to plant the seeds, summer is the time to watch and make sure the conditions and environment are appropriate for growth, and fall is harvest season where farmers reap the reward of their efforts. Next is winter; a time to rest the soil, take care of the farm and machinery, and get ready to start all over again. The Bible often uses farming as a metaphor for proper order and timing in life, and it teaches us that there is a specific time and season for everything.

> *There is a time for everything,*
> *and a season for every activity*
> *under the heavens.*
>
> Ecclesiastes 3:1 (NIV)

We all experience different seasons in our lifetime. Each season is different, beautiful in its own way, and most importantly, it has its own specific purpose. Just as the farmer can't skip a step in his process to reap a rich harvest, neither can you skip the learning and growing process to reap the blessings and fruits of your labor.

Life is a built-up, never-ending process of learning, growing, and becoming better. There is always something to learn and room to expand ourselves. You are either flourishing and growing in life, or you are dying. God does have a plan and a purpose for your life, and the journey of becoming the person He has destined for you to become is more important than the destination itself. Those who focus on results can become disillusioned by the constant chase for accomplishment or become disheartened when their idea of success does not come to pass. In contrast, those who focus on growing better every day prepare themselves for whatever life throws at them, including opportunities they might not have seen or been prepared to embrace otherwise.

Focus on the process, not the result. Results are a natural byproduct of remaining disciplined in the process. Focusing on the process prepares and equips you to receive what is next for you. God never gives you a desire or dream without equipping you to attain it. Staying aligned with the word of God, spending time in his presence, and listening to and obeying his directions will determine the speed of your blessing coming to pass.

> *"And we know that in all things God works for the good of those who love him, who have been called according to his purpose."*
>
> Romans 8:28 (NIV)

Navigating Every Season

Understanding your season of life is essential to focusing on and enjoying the present moment and what matters most in this season. I remember the first time I had the desire to come to the USA. I was 15 years old, and although I had no idea how that would happen, I just knew it would. The feeling and excitement of that "knowing" stayed with me. I never shut down that dream or allowed others' voices to shut it down either. For the next seven years, and in each season accordingly, I lived my life getting ready and making decisions that would bring me closer to my desire to come to the USA. The little steps you take are moving you closer and closer to what you want. Don't give up. I started saving money and searching for opportunities to make my dream happen.

I was twenty-two years old when I finally came to the USA for the first time. It was an amazing experience! I remember my flight, my arrival, the smell, the scenery, and the punch of Arizona heat in August. I loved it all! I also remember attending the church where my cousin was the worship pastor and feeling at home. Everything was new and different from what I had experienced in life to that point.

THE JOY OF BECOMING

I grew up catholic, and the God I knew was more like an Old Testament God. In the U.S. I was introduced to a loving and caring God, a graceful and merciful father that loved me and met me where I was. It was a big shift in my mind towards God. I sure had a long way to go in learning and growing close to God, but that trip spending six months in Phoenix, Arizona changed what I wanted for my future as I spent time learning and growing closer to God.

I didn't want to go back to Brazil, but my visa was up, and I didn't have a choice. When I got back to Brazil, I felt lost. Something inside of me had changed, and I no longer fit there. I remember a couple of my close friends telling me I was different; I was not the same girl who left 6 months before. I could sense a change as well, and I was encouraged by the possibilities of whom I could become by spending more time in America and more time with a God who loved me and had big plans for me. I immediately started searching for what would bring me back to America again.

I found my way back to Phoenix six months later. I was so happy again, and God created ways for me to have fresh experiences that made my time there even better. I was given the chance to visit Hawaii with a friend of my cousin, and I was blown away by the beauty of God's majesty on display while there. However, while visiting Maui I lost my passport and visa, and my plans of staying longer ended. I was devastated. I could not understand why all that was happening. I thought living in America was God's plan for my future, but obstacles continued to find their way on my path. At the time, I could not see another way for me to come back again.

However, God had a bigger and better plan for me and my future; a much better plan than the one I had and was trying to make happen on my own. I see now that I needed to grow, humble myself, and give up control in that season. I needed to enjoy the process and learn my lessons no matter what I was going through. Again, I was learning to obey God's guidance, plans, and timing.

THE JOY OF BECOMING

> *"Now to Him who is able to do exceedingly, abundantly above all that we ask or think, according to the power that works in us"*
>
> Ephesians 3:20 (NKJV)

In January 2009, I went back to Brazil frustrated and sad. I got back to doing what I knew I could do at the time. I started working as a business consultant with a cousin and got into the restaurant business with my father. I kept myself busy with work and seeking God, even though I didn't understand why I had to be there. Deep inside I knew there was a reason, so I decided to make the most out of it and focused on learning and growing professionally.

The waiting period sometimes means a development period, where you are getting prepared and ready for what is to come next. Nevertheless, it can also be a challenging period when nothing makes sense. The pieces might not come together to bring about what God has promised you in exactly the way you expect but remember that God is always working all things together for your good and His glory. He wants His glory to be shown *in* your life so that His glory can be shown *through* your life!

While working as a consultant, we needed to fill a position for one of our clients. The girl we hired had participated in an exchange program to work at Disney World, and she told me about an Au Pair exchange program where girls come to the U.S. and live with an American family and work as a nanny for them while experiencing the culture and going to school as well! I loved talking with her and sharing our experiences in America. Talking to her also sparked my hope and excitement about the possibility of once again coming to live in the U.S.

I decided to go to an agency and check out the Au Pair program without telling anyone in my family, as I knew they would not be very happy with my decision. I remember that day so well. It was my birthday, April 18th, 2010, and it was like the start of a new life for me. I got to the agency, learned about the program, signed up, filled out all the paperwork, and just like that I had my profile online to find my matching family. I left the agency so excited that I skipped the streets of Sao

Paulo. I was also anxious about telling my parents, as I knew that they would not be very excited about me leaving for another country again. But I needed to do something for myself, my future, and my happiness. The kind of life I was living in Brazil was not at all what I wanted for my life.

When the time is right, everything just works fast and perfectly. Three months after skipping out of the exchange agency's office, in July 2010, I was boarding a plane for a week of training in New Jersey and then on a plane to San Diego, California to meet my host family, with which I would be living for the next two years. God's plans are always bigger and better than what you can think or understand! I ended up living in San Diego for almost eight years, and it was an amazing experience! I learned and grew so much.

After the Au Pair program ended and I was forced to return to Brazil once more, I quickly found my way into an MBA program in San Diego, which fulfilled another vision I had for a while. This allowed me to return to America once more and further my education, and I was able to continue living with and working for the same family that hired me as an Au Pair. About a year into my two-year MBA program, I met the most amazing man! He was the one God has been preparing for me, the love of my life. Marrying him a year later also meant that my stay in America would finally be permanent!

I want you to see in my story how important is to understand the season of life you are in. Find things to be grateful for and be open to learning and growing. Recognize there is a reason for everything and never give up on your dreams or the promises God has made to you. Even when everything and everyone around you tells you otherwise.

> *"Always give yourselves fully to the work of the Lord, because you know that your labor in the Lord is not in vain."*
>
> 1 Corinthians 15:58 (NIV)

Nothing you do can escape the eyes of the Lord. I want to encourage you to take the steps I'm teaching you in this book; identify your season, and what is important now. At all times, lean closer to God, be obedient, and let all that you do be done with love for Him. Continue believing and having faith, and at the right time, his promises will come to pass, and it will be better than anything you have imagined!

Time for Reflection: Consider the following questions as they relate to your season of life:

1. What is most important in the season of life you are in now?

2. What adjustments do you need to make to fully enjoy this season?

3. How can you embrace and enjoy the changes of this season?

8. Declutter Your Life

Do you have a space, room, or drawer in your house or office where you put all the things you think you will need later? You know that place that is now full of all the things you will never touch again. Maybe you have a mess you know you need to organize or clean up, but you keep telling yourself "I'll get to it later."

Do you know that cluttered spaces and unresolved circumstances can cause you to experience energy leaks? An energy leak is when you can't fully focus all your energy on one task because your mind keeps running and reminding you of all the unresolved, unfinished, unattended tasks, ideas or things you have in the back of your mind causing you to feel frustrated and consequently run down.

Beyond a physical energy leak, you can also experience an emotional energy leak which is brought about by unresolved or unforgiven matters in a relationship, like offenses and traumas you experienced but never fully dealt with. Consequently, you keep reviving, thinking, worrying, and obsessing over that matter and you can't let go of it. Regardless of its root or specific manifested form, energy leaks can draw essential power away from you and steal your ability to accomplish your mission.

It is important to clean up the clutter you have in your life and remove the weight of the unresolved things nurturing the feelings of stress, lack of control, or failure you may be feeling. Whatever is keeping you stuck and robbing you of living a free and joyful life needs to be identified and eliminated. When you continue to hold on to either physical or emotional energy leaks, you'll keep looking back and reliving what happened in the past, preventing you from moving forward and opening space for what God wants to bring into your life.

A common source of energy leaks is physical or mental messes brought on by taking on too much and not properly planning to ensure everything has a place and gets put in its place. I tend to get distracted, overwhelmed, and restricted in crowded spaces with too many things and people. I aspire to keep my house and my surroundings as open and clean as possible, with lots of natural light and fresh air, so I can think better and have a peaceful mind and mood. I'm constantly looking around for energy leaks that might be distracting me and slowing me down.

As a mom, I had to learn to be okay with toys around the house and common messes kids leave in their wake. After becoming an entrepreneur and working from home, I also had to learn to be okay with not taking care of the house chores all day. I had to create a schedule to help me manage my time and all my responsibilities. I can declutter my mind by organizing my agenda and setting a specific time for each task I want to accomplish like chores, work, cleaning, serving, my date with God, exercising, resting, having fun with my kids, and spending time with my husband.

As I open space in my mind from constantly having to remind myself of each task I must do during my day, I'm able to focus and be more productive in the time I have set to accomplish each task. Discipline is freedom! As I discipline myself to schedule my time effectively and stick to the schedule, I allow myself to be fully present and enjoy each moment knowing that all my responsibilities are scheduled and saved in my calendar, and I will be reminded of each one before it's time for it. I no longer experience the energy leaks that come from worrying about missing something or forgetting to do something important. When my calendar is full and there is more to do, I prioritize and either delegate, postpone or eliminate what doesn't make the priority list. Again, this is simple, but not easy. It is something that I have had to practice consistently to master.

Another significant source of clutter with far-reaching mental and emotional impacts is unforgiveness. Forgiving others might be the hardest thing you ever do, but it could be the most freeing thing you ever do as well. There is an adage that says, "unforgiveness is like drinking poison and expecting the other person to die," and another one that says, "unforgiveness is like setting yourself on fire and expecting the other person to die from smoke inhalation." Refusing to forgive and harboring resentment only harms you. The Bible talks so much about forgiveness, because it is essential to our well-being. By releasing our need to be vindicated over how others have treated us, we free ourselves from carrying the emotional weight that comes with bitterness and resentment. As my husband once wrote in a poem,

> *"I forgive you.*
>
> *Not because you've earned it or deserve it,*
>
> *But because I need to be freed,*
>
> *From the burden."*
>
> "Forgiveness" by James W. Collins

The Bible teaches us to forgive as our heavenly father has forgiven us.

> *"Forgive as the Lord forgave you."*
> Colossians 3:13 (NIV)

Forgiveness does not mean forgetting, minimizing the offense, reconciling with the offender, or allowing it to happen again. It is a daily choice you must make to free yourself from the foothold the devil is using against you through the circumstance. I invite you to take time and think about any areas of unforgiveness you might be carrying. Pray about this and ask the Holy Spirit to reveal to you the people and circumstances that you need to forgive and release.

This is simple, but simple isn't always easy. As hard as it might be, I promise you it will be worth it.

Sometimes the people you need to forgive are no longer in your life, or you no longer have a relationship or desire to contact that person. The absence of the person from your life does not eliminate the need for you to forgive them. Trust me, I know this can be very emotional and difficult. Often, the people we need to forgive most are people that have hurt us badly, and even thinking about that person or the events they are involved in is emotionally taxing. However, failure to explore the events and people involved that leads to forgiveness will leave you in bondage.

A useful practice for forgiveness is to write a letter to the person (or people) you need to forgive. Take your time reflecting on what you have been harboring about the person and write as if you were writing directly to them. Say everything you need to say that maybe you haven't had the courage, or never had the chance to say to them. Get it all out. Allow yourself to feel every emotion that naturally arises. Then write that you forgive them, truly release any remaining resentment you carry, and then pray for them. You can choose to send the letter to the person if you want, and if you desire to repair a relationship with them, but the other person doesn't have to read it for you to get the benefit. Just the act of writing is enough for you to process the emotions you are carrying and discharge the negative energy associated with the people and events involved. Tear the letter and throw it away or burn it in a fire if you so choose. Either way, you will feel lighter, and your heart will be cleansed of the bitterness that cripples your potential.

I would never advise you to do something I haven't done myself or aren't willing to do myself. I have had to work on decluttering my heart from all the layers of scars, damages, traumas, and aches I have built up from my past. I realized there were things I kept holding onto and allowing to distract, weigh me down, and control my feelings and actions. By forgiving the ones who once hurt me and receiving God's forgiveness for my own past sins, I was able to experience freedom like never before. During the forgiveness process, I learned it was easier for me to forgive others than it was to forgive myself.

Can you relate to that? I had high expectations for myself and the goal to be perfect, which is obviously impossible. This did not serve me well. Since I was harsh with myself, I never felt good enough, I was not able to celebrate my accomplishments, and I was not able to enjoy anything due to such impossible standards I would never be able to meet.

I remember after marrying James and becoming a mom, I learned that there is no such thing as perfection. Together, he and I set new standards and goals for ourselves, and my focus switched from achieving perfection to achieving excellence instead. I was able to shift my expectation of wanting to be perfect to thriving to be excellent, which means I give my absolute best in anything and everything I do. That is a goal I can measure and achieve, and it is a much healthier perspective to maintain!

Just that shift of expectation made a big difference in my life. A heavyweight I carried about myself, and others were lifted. It helped me improve my relationship with myself, my husband, and everyone around me as I quit expecting perfection from myself and others. I'm constantly praying and asking God to reveal to me the circumstances, feelings, or relationships I need to work on or release to Him, and that He will give me wisdom and strength to change the things I can control and surrender to him the things I can't.

Now I want to invite you to think about the unresolved things or relationships you have going on in your own life, the things running in the back of your mind and causing energy leaks for you. Make a list of what you need to declutter. Also, pray and ask God to reveal anything you might be missing that needs to go and ask Him to give you wisdom and strength to take the necessary actions to resolve it. Also, make a list of the people you need to forgive, no matter how big or small the matter is. Then pray for them, bless them, and do good to them. Make the choice to not repay evil for evil, be in peace with everyone, and leave room for God to handle the circumstances you can't.

> *"Do not be overcome by evil,*
> *but overcome evil with good."*
> Romans 12:21 (NIV)

Declutter Your Life

I pray that you will make the choice and have the strength to declutter your life, body, soul, and spirit. I pray that God will expose all that you need to let go of and give you the power and good judgment to obey, surrender, and forgive all that is holding you captive from living the life God intends for you to live. I pray that as you open space in your heart, it will be filled with the Holy Spirit. As you open space in your life, new blessings will come in, and you will experience freedom and peace that surpasses all understanding, in Jesus's name. Amen!

If you are struggling to identify some things that need focus or need to be resolved in your life, find a quiet place, bring a notebook with you, close your eyes, and take a few deep breaths. Just focus on breathing for a minute. You will notice your mind trying to bring up all the things needed to be resolved. Take note of the things that are popping up in your mind and then schedule a time to work on each one. You can also take this time to practice the letter-writing exercise I spoke about earlier to forgive the people you need to forgive. Imagine as you are burning or throwing the letter away if you don't decide to give it to the person, that you are laying it all at the feet of Jesus. This action is a representation to yourself that it is finished, and it is washed by the blood of Jesus. Accept and surrender that Jesus is taking it from you. You don't need to carry this pain any longer.

> *"In your anger do not sin."*
> *Do not let the sun go down while you are still angry, and do not give the devil a foothold.*
> Ephesians 4:26-27 (NIV)

When the enemy tries to bring that up again and use it against you, you can say with authority right back at him "The (situation, person, or feeling) that you once used against me to keep me stuck and isolated no longer has any power over me and my life. I've laid it down at the feet of Jesus, and it has been washed by his blood." Notice, that I said "when" and not "if." The devil is real. He studies you well, he knows your weaknesses, and he will use everything he can to destroy you. Be ready and strong in the word and know the truth to protect yourself against his lies.

Now I invite you to find that quiet place I referenced before and answer the questions on the following page for yourself. This is the beginning of your journey to declutter and open space in your mind, heart, and life for all the amazing blessings God has prepared for you!

Time for Reflection: Consider the following questions as they relate to the things you must let go of.

1. What is out of your control that you need to surrender to God?

2. What have you lost and not properly mourned/grieved that keeps coming back to you?

3. Who/what do you need to forgive?

PART III

Your Path to

New Life

9. Your Identity

Your identity is a determining factor for everything you will experience and achieve in life. The dictionary defines identity as the specific characteristics (i.e., belief systems, facts, behaviors, habits, and preferences) that determine who you are. In the context of what your life means on this planet, nothing is more important than understanding who you are. Establishing your identity enables you to simultaneously understand who you are in this moment while confidently projecting who you can become!

When your identity is rooted in Christ, you can walk boldly in your purpose because you fully accept who God says you are. He says you are His precious child! He created you in His image, and He so loved you He gave His only son to wash away your sins so you could be in a relationship with Him. You are forgiven and accepted in your own uniquely beautiful broken way. Consider the following Bible verses to verify what God's word says about you:

Your Identity

> *Therefore, if anyone is in Christ, the new creation has come: The old has gone, the new is here!*
>
> 2 Corinthians 5:17 (NIV)

> *So God created man in His own image; in the image of God He created him; male and female He created them.*
>
> Genesis 1:27 (NKJV)

> *But as many as received Him, to them He gave the right to become children of God, to those who believe in His name.*
>
> John 1:12 (NKJV)

> *For God so loved the world that He gave His one and only Son, that whoever believes in Him shall not perish but have eternal life.*
>
> John 3:16 (NIV)

> *Before I formed you in the womb I knew you, before you were born, I set you apart.*
>
> Jeremiah 1:5 (NIV)

> *For you created my inmost being you knit me together in my mother's womb. I praise you because I am fearfully and wonderfully made; your works are wonderful*
>
> Psalm 139: 13-14 (NIV)

Your Identity

Every believer gets to claim these truths about their identity, but God has given you specific strengths, beliefs, gifts, and talents to build you up and empower you to love, accept and celebrate your uniqueness. Too often people associate their identity with a single aspect of their life, such as their job or relationships (i.e., wife, mother, friend, etc.). Let me tell you, you are bigger than your job title or relational title! If you are walking in your purpose, then your gifts will benefit you and the people around you in these areas of life, but these things do not define you!

It is important to understand if your identity is attached to a single aspect of your life because if you lose that thing, you will lose yourself and have a major identity crisis. Likewise, the deeper an idea or belief you have is attached to your identity, the harder it will be for you to grow if that belief or idea doesn't sustain your next level. As long as you stay attached to that as part of your identity, you will stay exactly where you are. However, when your identity is rooted in God, you can embrace your differences, unique gifts, strengths, and weaknesses as qualities and skills that qualify you to fulfill your calling. Seeing yourself as God sees you, wonderfully and fearfully made, will give you the confidence to faithfully step into the calling God has placed on your life so you can touch and change lives in a way that only you can.

I really want you to see the positive correlation between your identity and the ability to fulfill God's purpose for your life. The more you know who you are and whose you are, the faster you will overcome the fears and insecurities you experience. I can encourage you in this from my own struggles with fear and insecurity. I now have the right tools, my identity, and faith in the word of God, to fight those feelings that once robbed me of doing what God was calling me to.

I have experienced the feeling of losing my identity a few times in my life. The last time was when I entered motherhood. I understand now that it had nothing to do with my beautiful kids, but with my way of thinking and the expectations I had of myself and others. My strong, independent, and observant self, used to think I could do it all on my own. My way was the best and most efficient way of doing things. After becoming a mom, my fear of losing my loved ones grew tremendously as I had this precious and beautiful baby as my responsibility. It was not just me anymore.

Your Identity

In order to alleviate my fears, I tried to control everything. Looking back, I can see and understand that subconsciously I believed that if I always had control of the situation nothing bad could happen to my babies. As a result, I became an over-protective mother. I believed I was doing the best thing for my kids, and that I could protect them from pain. Now I can clearly see that the fear and controlling mindset I carried had been embedded in me as a child from my experiences through certain traumas, in addition to the fear passed down from my mom and my grandma from the things they had experienced.

The limiting belief of control was created to protect me, and it served me for a season. However, as I entered marriage and motherhood, it no longer served me. It was harming myself, my kids, and my relationship with my husband. It became a heavy burden I carried around thinking I had to manage and handle every second of my kids' lives. It was exhausting, scary, and overwhelming. It was clearly affecting my life and my relationships.

As I prayed for God to help me, He met me where I was and started revealing to me a generational spirit of fear robbing me and my family from living the life God intended for us to live. And I had to break it once and for all. God brought the right resources into my life once I was ready to ask for them and receive them. I took advantage of every opportunity He presented, and I was ready and eager to work on myself. My eyes were opened to see the changes I needed to make. It was the beginning of another shift in my beliefs. I learned that fear is a spirit, and it does not come from God. Verse 2 Timothy 1:7 became my weapon against the spirit of fear every time it tried to torment my mind.

> *"For God has not given us a spirit of fear, but of power and of love and of a sound mind."*
> 2 Timothy 1:7 (NKJV)

Finding my identity in Christ, and what it meant to live that out, gave me the courage and confidence to go after the desires of my heart. Having the faith I need to live in the freedom and joy Jesus paid the ultimate price for me to experience prepares me to fearlessly face the challenges in my way, and it can do the same for you!

Your Identity

The first step toward understanding who you are in Christ is to get to know God better. The best way to get to know God is to read His word and talk to Him daily. Schedule your daily date with God. What is the best time for you to start digging into His word? If you have never done it, please don't feel intimidated by the Bible. I'm saying this because I have felt intimidated and thought I would never understand the Bible. That thought didn't do anything for me, other than keep me from growing closer to God.

The most important thing is to START! You can start reading Proverbs, or a book in the New Testament, explore different translations, or pick a daily devotional to start that will assist you in understanding the message and becoming more familiar with the Bible. Make it a priority and be consistent. Show up to your date with God with an open mind and expectation of encountering His amazing love and grace and enjoy discovering your identity in Him!

Now I want to talk to you about your uniqueness. You have characteristics, skills, and natural talents that set you apart from everyone else. Not better than everyone else, but unique from everyone else. In his book, *Your Divine* Fingerprint, my pastor, Keith Craft, explains it like this: "God has given you a fingerprint that nobody else has so you can leave an imprint that nobody else can leave." God has endowed you with gifts and talents that are unique to you and are designed to serve you in serving Him, through serving others.

You might be thinking right now that you don't have any gifts. Let me assure you, that you have many! Have you ever been complimented by someone about a character trait, skill, or ability that you possess? This likely points to a unique gift God has given you. Often, we take these gifts for granted because it's easy to think, "well, that's just who I am," or "that comes so easily for me, it must come easy for everyone." The fact is, what comes easy to you does not come easy to everyone, and what comes easy to you is a sign of natural gifts and talents God has given you to serve His purpose for you on earth.

I understand if you cannot think of anything right now. It might be hard for you to identify your own gifts if you have never thought about them before, or if you

Your Identity

believe you are bragging about yourself if you do so. Since these gifts come so easily to you, and you have been succeeding in these things your whole life, you might not see them as gifts. I'm here to tell you that they are your most special gifts from God, and he gave you those gifts so you can reach, and touch others' lives like no one else can.

If you have a hard time identifying your gifts on your own, as I had before, you might just need a second set of eyes to help you see them. Here is what you can do: reach out to a close friend, your partner, or another family member that knows you well and ask them to point out your gifts, the things that are unique to you, and how you impact others in a positive way. To make sure you get the answer you are expecting, here is an example of how you can ask for help clarifying your gifts and uniqueness. Say, "Hey <u>(Name of the person)</u> I'm looking to identify the gifts God has given me. I know very well my weaknesses and biggest struggles. Right now, I need to clarify my unique gifts to fulfill the purpose God intends for my life. Since you know me well, and you watch how I live my life in this world, would you please help give me a better understanding of my God-given gifts?

THE JOY OF BECOMING

As the Bible explains, your gifts were given to you so you can serve others the way only you can.

> *Each of you should use whatever gift you have received to serve others, as faithful stewards of God's grace in its various forms.*
> 1 Peter 4:10 (NIV)

When you have a clear understanding of what sets you apart, you can embrace your uniqueness, and you use your story and testimony to love and serve others. Knowing your strengths helps you to focus on developing those more and more as you work to live out your God-given potential. It is easy for most of us to focus on our weaknesses or the things that don't come naturally to us in an attempt to be good at everything and eliminate weaknesses or shortcomings. The problem is, you weren't designed to be perfect or good at everything. You are different for a reason, and you have unique skills and talents for a reason. You are much better served by focusing on developing your

Your Identity

strengths in order to mitigate your weaknesses, rather than focusing on your weaknesses and neglecting the parts of your identity that empower you to prosper on your mission.

As you begin to identify, embrace, and cultivate your gifts, everything around you will change for the better because you will be operating as your best self. You will notice your marriage gets better, your relationships, in general, will improve, and you will see positive changes in your career as well. You will have so much joy to spread around while feeling fulfilled in everything you do.

When you don't know your identity and gifts, you are vulnerable to labels you or others can put on yourself to describe you or something you are facing. They are not the truth about you and who you are. Now is the time for you to let go of any label you have picked up for yourself, or someone else has put on you, that comes against God's truth about who you are. Any label that might have been giving you a false sense of identity, or your past experiences does not define who you are and it needs to be consciously released.

THE JOY OF BECOMING

The way you behave is also a big part of your identity. This includes how you act, how you conduct yourself, and how you respond to what happens in your daily life. The cognitive behavior triangle explains that

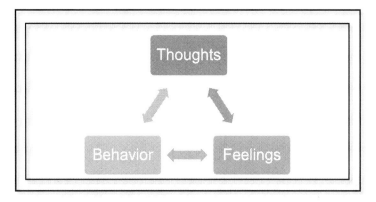

your thoughts impact the way you feel, which triggers a specific behavior, which in turn triggers more thoughts, feelings, and behaviors in a constant cycle.

This cycle is largely responsible for the value of your life, the impact of your life, and the level of fulfillment you experience in life. The feelings that are evoked by your thoughts are powerful determinants of how you act, and how you act means everything in the context of what your life will mean and what you will get out of life.

The more your thoughts are aligned with your values, God's word, and your identity in Him, the more

Your Identity

your actions will align with what you value most. It is a cycle that builds upon itself and can be a very powerful tool to help you become everything God has created you to be. However, the opposite is also true. The more incongruent your thoughts are with the values and identity you desire to possess, the further and further you will stray from becoming the best version of yourself. Whatever you think about manifests in life through your feelings and actions, so that you become what you think about the most.

Therefore, if you change the way you think, you can change your behavior. If you change your behavior, you will change your life. As I mentioned before, awareness is the key to change and growth. When you can clearly see the behaviors that no longer serve you, you can choose to make the changes necessary to transform and flourish.

The desires of our flesh induce strong emotions that will dictate our actions if we allow them to. For this reason, the Bible talks about not living by your flesh but being led by the spirit and God's laws.

> *For the flesh desires what is contrary to the Spirit, and the Spirit what is contrary to the flesh. They are in conflict with each other, so that you are not to do whatever you want.*
> Galatians 5:17 (NIV)

One of my core values is gratitude, and it is not because I'm always grateful, but because I choose to be. I can naturally be very negative; my mind can very quickly see all the things going wrong around me at any point in time. I decided that I didn't want to be that person, and I chose to make a change in myself to realign my thoughts to focus on the positive instead of the negative. I learned that If I wanted to become a grateful person, I would need to modify my way of thinking. I started a gratitude journal routine, and the intentional and simple exercise of writing three things I was grateful for every day has helped me shift my focus to look for the good in everything, and consequently, shift my heart to be more grateful.

Your Identity

> *"Watch and pray so that you will not fall into temptation. The spirit is willing, but the flesh is weak."*
>
> Matthew 26:41 (NIV)

When I became aware of my lack of appreciation for all the blessings I had in my life, I could then do something to change. Before I didn't think I was being negative, that is just how I lived. However, once it was revealed to me, I knew that behavior was not aligned with God's word and the life I want to live. I quickly decided to start acting my way into becoming a grateful person.

What I hope you learn from my experience is that if you are not experiencing the life you want, it is time to choose a different path. You have the power to choose a better life! Your experiences are the results of the choices you make. Happiness is not a result of what you have. It does not come from another person, a place, or something you are doing. It is your thoughts that will make you feel happy or unhappy in any circumstance.

If you are not living out your identity and not seeing the fruit you want to see in all areas of your life, take a different approach. God's approach. You have nothing to lose. To do this, you need to learn His way, by reading and studying His word in the Bible, and grow stronger in Him every day.

> *"The mind governed by the flesh is death, but the mind governed by the Spirit is life and peace."*
> Romans 8:6 (NIV)

Do not be afraid of changing, reinventing, trying, and experiencing new things. It is never too late for you to start becoming the person you were created to be. You are also constantly changing and evolving, and if you have breath in your lungs, NOW is the best time to start moving in the direction of your destiny! Focus on what you can control, your attitude and actions, and surrender to God all that you can't control. Your fears and limiting beliefs are not your identities. Reinvent yourself by understanding the gifts that set you apart,

Your Identity

embrace your uniqueness, and make the choice to live out your God-given potential!

Time for Reflection: Consider the following questions as they relate to your identity to help you be specific with what that means to you:

1. Who are you really? What is your identity?

2. What labels have you accepted that are not aligned with what God says about you?

3. What are your unique gifts and talents?

10. Renew Your Mind

> *"Do not conform to the pattern of this world but be transformed by the renewing of your mind. Then you will be able to test and approve what God's will is— his good, pleasing and perfect will."*
>
> Romans 12:2 (NIV)

Your mind is what enables you to be self-aware and conscious of the world around you. It manifests as thoughts, feelings, memories, imagination, will, and sensation. Your mind controls so much of your daily life, yet you likely spend very little time thinking about what you think about. Many of your actions and reactions are automatic decisions your mind makes to respond based on neural pathways that have been established over time through continuous repetition.

THE JOY OF BECOMING

While I don't pretend to be an expert, I've learned enough about how our brains work to know that, unless you are intentional about identifying how you think and why you think what you think, you will be unable to take advantage of a superpower that God has blessed you with. Through a process called neuroplasticity, you can retrain your brain to think and react in a deliberate and purposeful way. You don't have to be led by old ways of thinking that will keep you stuck in the same habits and behaviors that prevent you from performing at your peak. Through discipline, you can rewire your brain and create brand-new neural pathways that better support your growth and ideal state of being. If you want to learn more about this from an actual expert, I highly recommend the book *Switch on Your Brain* by Dr. Caroline Leaf.

When you realize you have the power to control your mind and the way you think, you will gain freedom unlike any you've experienced before. What you do with that freedom is up to you, but if you are mindful and intentional, you can literally recreate your experience of life from the inside out. Too often, we can allow the desire for comfort or deep-rooted pride and beliefs to keep us stuck in patterns of thinking that limit our potential. There is always room for growth, and if you keep an open mind to continue learning, growing, and developing yourself, you will achieve more than you could ever imagine.

To illustrate, allow me to tell you a recent story from my own life. 2021 ended very differently than I expected. I started feeling sick on Christmas eve when my whole family got COVID, and I was out for over 5 days. My husband and I had planned some fun events for us and the kids, and we had scheduled time to dream and set goals together for the new year. However, since we had the virus, we isolated ourselves as he and I barely functioned enough to keep ourselves and the kids fed and somewhat comfortable. All those plans we had to have fun as a family, as a couple, and to dream about the possibilities that awaited in 2022 went down the drain.

On New Year's Eve, I found myself discouraged and upset. My thoughts started spiraling in the wrong direction. I started listing all the things that didn't work the way I wanted in 2021, and those thoughts kept me captive feeling hopeless and sorry for myself. I allowed myself to be in that state of mind for a couple of days.

I felt hopeless, and I hate to feel hopeless. But I believe God allows things in our lives so we can learn from them and give Him space to show up and remind us that He is in control.

I'm a strong and determined woman. I go after what I want, and I have faith and a strong relationship with God. I'm also an imperfect human, and this experience has helped me reevaluate the expectations I created for myself. It also reminded me that God has a bigger plan, and as long as I'm following his guidance and putting him in the center of all, everything will work together for my good.

> *"We take captive every thought to make it obedient to Christ."*
> 2 Corinthians 10:5 (NIV)

To recenter and get back to my senses, I had to first recognize what was going on. My thoughts were creating a false sense of reality. The reality was, I had an amazing year in 2021 with many blessings for my family, so much personal and professional growth, and new opportunities that held promise for my future. I started my own business as a life coach, I served others like never before, and I was able to impact so many lives.

I made a choice to get myself out of that state of mind and take control of my thoughts. I went back to my "why," my values, and my purpose in life. The reason why I do anything and everything. I had to dig deep into my faith and remember that God has a great plan for my life, and his timing is perfect. I can't see the big picture, but He can. It reminded me of what the Bible says about faith.

> *"Now faith is confidence*
> *In what we hope for*
> *and assurance about*
> *what we do not see."*
> Hebrews 11:1 (NIV)

I also had to talk about it, be bold, and be willing to share what I was thinking and feeling. It was not easy, but I know how important that is. When I became mindful of my thoughts, it quickly became clear to me that I was focusing on the wrong things.

THE JOY OF BECOMING

I believe God led me through this experience so I can share and help others that might be struggling today. I want you to know that life is not perfect, and we all struggle. However, you can choose to view your circumstances from a different perspective, with an open mind, and decide to take control of your life and keep moving forward.

The fact that you woke up today means God is not done with you! He loves you, and He will work all things together for your good and his glory. Be open to receiving the revelations you need and review your thoughts and beliefs. Your job is to have faith and belief. God's job is to make it happen.

As you begin this journey of mindfulness, it is important to remember that your eyes and your ears are the entryways to your mind. Everything you see and hear feeds your mind and influences your thoughts and consequently your feelings. What shows you watch on TV, the movies you expose yourself to, social media content, music, podcast, and radio programs you listen to all have a direct correlation to the way you currently think and feel.

The more you feed your mind with negativity, tragedy, bad news, and the ways of this world, the more you will feel fear, anxiety, sadness, hopelessness, and depression. The more you feed your mind with the word of God, positivity, and good news, the more you will strengthen your faith and feel hope, peace, and joy that comes from God and surpasses all understanding. I've learned that fear is a feeling that can get as strong as I allow it to. My feelings are driven by my thoughts, and my thoughts are driven by what I see, hear and believe. These feelings can hold me back from living my own life. How crazy is that?

I don't know about you, but my imagination is so creative when it comes to worst-case scenarios, especially if it is about my kids or the people I love. My mind seems to easily conjure up scenarios that scare me so badly, and the associated feelings can feel so real. It is like when you wake up from a nightmare shaking, and it takes a minute for you to realize it was just a dream and not reality. I have experienced irrational fear so strongly that I've developed panic attacks, and I don't wish that on anybody.

I have dealt with fear so much in my life, and after I became a mom, this feeling has grown even more. I remember times when I felt that If I allowed my crazy thoughts to keep going, I wouldn't even leave my house. I would just stay and hide from all the bad things that could happen to me or my kids out in the world. However, now I know that fear is a feeling that I can acknowledge and move beyond. I can choose not to entertain those thoughts for too long. I have learned to catch the thought as it rises up, take a few deep breaths, come back to reality and focus on what I can control now. The more I do that, the more powerless fear becomes over me, and the more automatic this response becomes over time.

I'm so grateful that I now understand more about fear, what it does, and how it affects me. I know that fear does not come from God, but the enemy uses it against me to hold me back from realizing the plans God has for my life.

This process of mindfulness and self-awareness has helped me to bring my fears to light, fight fear with the proper weapons, and to overcome and be set free from them. I have worked hard to break through fear in my life. I still experience fear every day, but now I have the tools to deal with it and continue to move toward the life God intends for me to live.

Another thing I learned to defeat fear is to be aware of what I'm feeding my mind every day. Whatever I allow into the environment of my mind will directly affect my thoughts, my feelings, and consequently my actions or lack of action. Remember your eyes and ears are the doors that direct access to your mind and soul. For that reason, be vigilant of what you allow into your mind and soul every day. If it does not serve your mission, it is not worth your time.

www.themariacollins.com

Time for Reflection: Consider the following questions as they relate to your actions as a product of your mindset.

1. Are your actions driven by your emotions?

2. How are you feeding your mind? Think about what you watch, read, listen to, and follow on social media. Is that adding any value to your life?

3. Write down your most scary thoughts and then reframe them with a positive faith-based thought.

11. Finding Your Joy

When was the last time you had some fun? Research has proven that having fun has a positive impact on our body and mood, combats stress, and strengthens relationships by helping create a connection with others. Simply put, being intentional about adding moments of fun to your life is a crucial element to you being your best!

Life can get pretty serious. Especially as a mom, I feel like there are so many things I must make sure are working properly, like making sure my kids are fed, clean, healthy, safe, and rested, and the list can go on and on. That's just talking about my kids. Then you add managing the house and business into the mix, serving with our church, and building relationships with others, and the responsibilities just keep growing. Even the number of times I have to say "no" or redirect a kid to something else, which I feel happens every three minutes, can make life intense when you have little ones running around.

THE JOY OF BECOMING

As my husband and I took on more to live out our mission and contribute at higher levels to the Kingdom of God, it put more pressure on us individually. I had to make a conscious choice to create space for fun in my life. For me with my little ones, this comes in the form of playing and enjoying the moment, and not worrying about the mess I would have to clean up later. I had to learn to allow my kids to express their creativity the way they wanted, and not the way I think is best. I also had to find time for fun with my husband and fun by myself. I *need* to have fun in my life, and every time I'm feeling overwhelmed and stressed, I'm usually not making time for FUN. In everything you do, you must include some fun. Whether at work, at school, as parents, as friends, or as partners. Otherwise, what's the point? The Bible says:

> *"A glad heart makes a cheerful face,*
> *but by sorrow of heart*
> *the spirit is crushed."*
>
> Proverbs 15:13 (ESV)

Finding Your Joy

When was the last time you gave yourself permission to play, laugh, and enjoy the moment? Making space for fun may not come easy for you, for several reasons. I want to set you free from whatever is robbing you of having some fun in your life. I want to encourage you to give yourself permission to have some fun!

Don't know how? No problem, I can relate. I remember when I finished my MBA and had more time to enjoy life, but because I had been so focused on studying and working, I forgot how to have fun. I even struggled to recall some of the things I once liked to do to play. Below is an approach I used that might help you as well:

1. Think of something fun you always wanted to do but haven't done yet; something that brings you excitement.
2. Would it be more enjoyable to do it with someone else? If so, who do you want to invite?
3. Schedule a date and time and invite the person you want to have some fun with. Even if it's fun by yourself, schedule time on your calendar for it, and just do it!

THE JOY OF BECOMING

As a coach, I love to help others accomplish what they want by asking powerful questions to fill the gap between their reality and their ideal. To start, I will usually ask:

1. What do you want and why do you want it? (Clarify your vision and understand your "why")
2. How can you achieve that? What steps do you need to take? (Create a plan)
3. What are the steps you will take first and by when? (Take action)

So now I encourage you to go plan the fun you are missing right now, enjoy every minute of it, and then do it again! Make it a consistent part of your life. Whatever that looks like for you, your family, and your lifestyle, you can experience more joy every day.

Something that has provided immense benefit to my life and allowed me to create an intentional space for joy every day is developing a morning routine. Over the last few years, I've read books, listened to podcasts, and learned from mentors and coaches, and one thing I've learned that almost all highly successful people have in common is a morning routine. Being intentional about planning how you start your day and developing the discipline to follow through on that plan will enable you to fill your cup first, so you are properly equipped to pour into others.

One of the things I've found that I must do for myself is to wake up before everyone else in my house so that I can enjoy a cup of coffee in peace and quiet, have my daily date with God, write in my gratitude journal, read my future letter and affirmations, and exercise. This morning routine brings me so much joy, energy, strength, and confidence to conquer my day. I will explore this further in hopes that it helps you develop your own morning routine that works to add joy to your life!

The first thing I do every morning after making my coffee is to retreat to my quiet space and read my Bible. It is so important to me that I give God the first moments of every day. I can do nothing outside of Him, and so I make Him first in my life every day by allowing Him to speak to and encourage me through His word. Currently, I am reading the Bible chronologically. However, there are many different approaches to reading the Bible, and I encourage you to find the method that works best for you. I usually find one or two verses that really speak to me each day, and I write those down in my journal and then start my gratitude practice.

Gratitude is a core value of mine because I understand the transformative power of maintaining a grateful heart. As I take the time every morning to think about all that I am grateful for, I'm intentionally focusing my mind on all the good I have now and what is to come. I chose this practice because I know that whatever I focus on will flourish in my life. Life can feel overwhelming at times but fixing my mind on the blessings I've been given helps to calm the storm and shift my perspective at any moment. An important Bible verse that I live by is found in 1 Thessalonians:

> *"Rejoice always, pray continually, give thanks in all circumstances;*
> *for this is God's will*
> *for you in Christ Jesus."*
> 1 Thessalonians 5:16-18 (NIV)

Finding Your Joy

Looking for things to be grateful for will absolutely shift your mood, thoughts, and attitude. Making gratitude a daily routine will transform your life.

After my gratitude practice, I read my letter from my future self. This is a powerful exercise that helps me visualize and feel the feelings of accomplishing all the things I desire in my heart to accomplish in the future. I wrote myself a letter from the future, which is dated a year from the time I wrote it, where I tell myself about all the amazing things that have happened to me and for me, my family, my business, my relationships, my health, and my finances in the past year. Then I have a list of affirmations and bible verses I speak over myself to remind me of who I am and whose I am.

> *"In every situation, by prayer and petition, with thanksgiving, present your requests to God. And the peace of God, which transcends all understanding, will guard your hearts and your minds in Christ Jesus. "*
>
> Philippians 4:6-7 (NIV)

THE JOY OF BECOMING

Finally, I pray. I enter God's presence with thanksgiving and ask for wisdom, discernment, guidance, protection, favor, prosperity, opportunities, alignments, boldness, and anything else that I need. I ask God to use me as his vessel in this world and allow me to shine his light onto others. I pray for my family, my friends, my clients, and any other person the Holy Spirit places in my heart.

What would it look like for you to add more joy to your days? What can you do to fill up your cup, beautiful? Don't be discouraged or overwhelmed if you don't know where to start. You can only start from where you are. It was a process for me, and it took time for me to find my best rhythm. Now that I have been strengthening those muscles, I'm able to find joy and be grateful in any situation more easily. It also required stretching my faith when everything around me strongly suggested that joy could not be found.

Finding Your Joy

> *"May the God of hope fill you*
> *with all joy and peace*
> *as you trust in him, so that*
> *you may overflow with hope*
> *by the power of the Holy Spirit."*
> Romans 15:13 (NIV)

God is faithful, and all his promises in Christ are YES and AMEN! He can do exceedingly, abundantly above all that you ask or think, and He is for you, always working all things together for your good and His glory. In every circumstance, you have the opportunity to choose stress or joy. Choose joy!

Time for Reflection: Consider the following questions as they relate to "Joy" to help you be specific with what that means to you:

1. What do you like to do for FUN? How often do you do that?

2. List the fun things you always wanted to do?

3. What can you do to fill up your cup every day?

12. Design Your Rhythm

You get to live one life here on earth, and you don't know when your expiration date is, so why not make the best out of it? Be intentional and create the life you want to have. It is possible by adding one new habit at a time. Many people underestimate what they can accomplish in 5 years, and overestimate what they can do in one year. New habits are created by repetition. You have to set yourself up for success by starting slowly, keeping track of your progress, and celebrating every little win. You are more likely to succeed and keep a new habit when you experience immediate reward or satisfaction.

Focus on the process of becoming. Your transformation is a journey that is meant to be enjoyed. By focusing on the process, it takes to achieve results rather than the results themselves, you will find that you are capable of achieving far more than you thought possible. Create a way to measure your progress like crossing days on your calendar, which will help you recognize your current and historical progress, so you can be reminded of how far you have come.

Establish a rhythm or routine that works best for you. It will be challenging at first, which is part of the process. In order to overcome the resistance at first while you are disciplining yourself, you must be consistent. You will need to act despite the discomfort, when you are not in the mood, despite doubt, despite the inconvenience, and despite fear.

When it becomes hard, and you feel like you can't do it anymore, remember to call on the name of Jesus and ask for the strength that comes from the Lord.

> *"I can do all things through Christ who strengthens me."*
> Philippians 4:13 (NKJV)

Give yourself grace and mercy and love yourself through the process. It is okay to fail, it is not ok to stay down. Pick yourself up, beautiful, shake it off, and keep moving.

Design Your Rhythm

Have you ever heard the saying "you cannot pour from an empty cup?" You might be feeling drained emotionally or physically like you don't have anything left to give to others. Or even feeling like you are not doing the things that once fulfilled you because you are too tired. As a wife, mom, kingdom builder, and entrepreneur, I'm always thinking about the needs of others and how to best serve and love them. Even though I love doing that, it can become exhausting for me at times. I have found myself discharged, emptied, and sad at times, not wanting to do the things that bring me joy, because I didn't feel like I had anything else to give.

I learned the importance of filling up my cup first by prioritizing rest and self-care in my daily routines, especially after having kids. And if I don't focus on myself first, I can't show up as my best self to serve others. I can't be the best example and mother I want to be for my kids when I'm impatient, unhappy, irritated, loud, and emotional.

Life can get busy, and things can get in my way throughout the day, so what works best for me is to make time for myself first thing in the morning, while my kids are still sleeping. Having a good night of sleep, getting quiet time, reading my Bible, writing in my gratitude journal, and exercising really helps me to love and care for myself and fulfill my heart before I need to serve anyone else. My morning discipline enables me to be prepared for whatever comes my way that day. If for some reason I skip my morning routine, I feel a bit lost during my day like something is missing, I also find myself more susceptible to losing my peace with circumstances or other people.

You are important, you are loved, you are worthy, and you are enough for your family, friends, coworkers, boss, or clients. The world needs you to show up at your best to give and serve with your gifts every day. Find what makes you happy and do something every day to fill up your cup. Be consistent and make yourself a priority. You cannot give what you don't have. Love yourself. Nurture your heart, as for out of the abundance of your heart your mouth speaks, and what you speak often finds a way to manifest itself into your life.

> *"A good man out of the good treasure of his heart brings forth good; and an evil man out of the evil treasure of his heart brings forth evil. For out of the abundance of the heart his mouth speaks."*
>
> Luke 6:45 (NKJV)

Choose your words wisely and speak kindly and lovingly to yourself. It is time to stop being so harsh to yourself and step into the authority God has given you. Start prophesying His truth over yourself, speak into life the promises of God, the things you want to see. If it is not going to bring any good, it is not worth saying.

> *"The tongue has the power of life and death"*
>
> Proverbs 18:21 (NIV)

As James, the brother of Jesus, explains in the verse below, your words are powerful, and whatever you speak impacts your whole body and the course of your life.

> *"It corrupts the whole body, sets the whole course of one's life on fire"*
> James 3:6 (NIV)

Watch the words you are speaking over yourself. Stop telling yourself you "can't" and find excuses for why you can't do something for yourself. Instead, ask the question, "what would it take for me to do this," or "what would need to happen for me to achieve that?" Stop the pattern and reverse it. Carefully and intentionally choose the words you want to come out of your mouth and watch how everything starts to shift in your favor!

By creating discipline and being consistent, I believe you can achieve anything you want. The Bible tells us to be prepared and continue the good works even when we are tired, or our efforts seem to us like they are not working.

> *"Therefore, my beloved brethren, be steadfast, immovable, always abounding in the work of the Lord, knowing that your labor is not in vain in the Lord."*
>
> 1 Corinthians 15:58 (NKJV)

This means you need to be prepared because there will be hard times in your journey. There will always be something getting in your way. The devil doesn't want you to succeed, and he works hard to stop you, isolate you, discourage you and make you think you are not enough or not worthy of living the life God intends for you to live.

Creating a plan will help you to focus and move towards your goals. However, if you don't act, you will never fulfill your God-given purpose. You need to give God something to work with by stepping out in faith and acting. Having an accountability partner to hold you accountable for following through is very helpful to start if you struggle with staying consistent. As a coach, that is one of my primary responsibilities, and you'll be amazed at how effective it is to have someone in your corner that can help you see your blind spots and guide you to stay on the straight and narrow path.

Another important fact to pay attention to when beginning something new is your environment or external factors. Here are a few ways that have helped me, and many of my clients, in making the implementation process easier and more maintainable:

1. Attach the new practice to something you already have as a habit. For example: if you want to take vitamins every day, you are more likely to succeed if you have your vitamins waiting for you when you finish brushing your teeth every morning.
2. Be prepared and don't think, just do it. For example: if you want to get up early to exercise, get your clothes ready the night before so you don't need to think of what you are going to wear. You can just get out of bed, get ready, and go. Much easier right? Well, if you have a hard

time getting out of bed, here is another tip. Set your alarm across the room. That way, you must get out of bed to turn it off before it wakes the whole house. Then you just need to change and move.

3. Set your environment up for success. For example, if you want a healthy diet, plan and prepare your meals and snacks ahead of time, and don't have unhealthy food around the house. Or if you want to focus and be productive, go to a quiet place and turn off any distractions.

4. Be intentional and smart about setting up the right time for each task you need to complete. For example, if you want to implement quiet time in your life, find the best time that works for your schedule. Set a reminder and make it a priority. If something else comes up, give yourself permission to say "no" to it.

It is also important to cut off the things and the people that are not aligned with your vision. It might seem harsh to you what I just said, but it is absolutely necessary. Surround yourself with like-minded individuals, the ones that will love you, respect you, help you grow, push you, and always lead you to God. Consistency and discipline will turn your dreams into reality. Stay focused, be flexible, and don't allow the distractions of life to steal you from living the life you want.

Time is one of the most precious assets you have. We all have the same amount of time every day, no matter who we are. What you choose to do and how you choose to use the time you have available will shape who you are, what you accomplish in life, and the kind of life you live. Once you know what matters the most to you, you can invest your time nurturing those things so you will experience the life you want and once prayed for.

Setting boundaries is a way to protect yourself and make better use of your time. You will be able to say "no" to the things that are not in alignment with what matters to you and the life you want to have by establishing clear boundaries for yourself and your time. Not every opportunity is a good opportunity. Trust me, I've struggled to say "no" before. As a result, I was too busy and could not find the time to care for myself or to focus on what I wanted to do. I remember the first time I heard that "no" is a complete sentence, it really hit me hard. I became aware that I was trying to please others and not loving and respecting myself in the process. I didn't have the time to focus on what I really wanted for myself.

As a coach, I remember being able to help one of my clients who struggled to say "no" to others. She had people-pleasing tendencies and avoided conflict at all costs. This didn't serve her. In fact, it made her feel out of control and upset every time she said "yes" to something she wanted to say "no" to. I coached her to think about boundaries; what it would look like to set healthy boundaries for herself, to protect her and make *her* needs her top priority, and how that would help her and make her feel.

She identified some healthy boundaries for herself, and immediately started applying them, and the transformation began. As she pushed herself to say "no" when she needed, she saw the reality that people accepted and respected her decision without question. With that, she created more time to focus and work on her goals and things that mattered to her. She also removed the pressure and weight she was carrying in trying to please others over herself.

What I want you to see, feel, and capture in this example is that the scenario you create in your head, your feelings, and the excuses you tell yourself to continue wasting your time, is not true. You are just trying to protect yourself and continue to stay in your comfort zone. You can start loving and respecting yourself by saying "no" when you need to and fighting the need to explain yourself. Again, it will be hard at first, but I know you can do it and benefit so much from it.

It was a couple of years ago that I learned and decided to apply the idea of adding everything to my calendar. I thought it was weird and not natural to schedule time for fun, resting, and spending quality time with loved ones. The reality is, if you don't set the time for the things that are important to you, you will end up not doing those things. There will always be something or someone putting demands on you and your time.

With all the responsibilities I have, managing my time well is so important, and it frees up my mind as well because I don't have to always be thinking about what I need to do. Every night or morning I can look at my calendar and get ready for my day. I know what to expect and the things I want to accomplish that day. As I began to follow my calendar, I got more things done, and I also learned to be flexible when the unexpected happens. This was a big lesson for me after becoming a mom.

Managing my time well and setting healthy boundaries helped me to take control of my time, free space, and energy to focus, be more productive and experience less stress. It led to me feeling more fulfilled and refreshed. You can take control of your time and life as well, find joy in any season with clarity in your goals and dreams, stop reacting to life and start acting towards what you want, and learn to appreciate what you have right now.

I hope and pray this book encourages you to follow the steps necessary for you to take control of your life once and for all. Learn and grow into the person God made you to be and boost your confidence to step faithfully into what God is calling you toward. Do this, and you will design and live the life God intends for you to live!

Time for Reflection: Consider the following questions as they relate to your every day to help you be specific with what you want it to be:

1. What is the rhythm/routine you want to have?

2. How can you set the right environment for your success?

3. How can you hold yourself accountable to follow through with the rhythm you want?

4. How are you going to overcome the obstacles that might show up?

ONE LAST MESSAGE

Congratulations Beautiful!!!

I'm so proud of you for choosing to improve yourself and experience the life God has for you here on earth!

My mission with this book was to encourage you to dream and envision the life you want, to remind you that you are God's Masterpiece created uniquely for a purpose and that you can do all things through Christ who strengthens you.

My hope is that you have become more excited and empowered to live your best life and are prepared to receive all the blessings God has for you.

Whether you live your best life and achieve your dreams is exclusively up to you. Nobody can guarantee your level of success, but when you have God by your side, all things become possible!

> "WITH MAN THIS IS IMPOSSIBLE,
> BUT WITH GOD ALL THINGS ARE POSSIBLE."
>
> Matthew 19:26

Special _FREE_ Bonus Gift for You

To help you achieve more success, get your **FREE BONUS RESOURCES** at:

www.TheMariaCollins.com

Download the Fast Action Workbook that accompanies this book to help you clarify your vision, experience freedom, and live with Passion, Purpose, and Prosperity.

ABOUT MARIA

Maria Collins is an exceptional wife, mother, friend, and Kingdom builder. She is an international coach, speaker, and best-selling author. She is passionate about helping women identify and live their true purpose and reach their God-given potential.

Leveraging an MBA and international business experience, Maria specializes in developing executives' mindsets and establishing successful strategies for winning in business and in life!

Her leadership has proven to produce results including helping multiple entrepreneurs launch new businesses, encouraging business owners to expand into new products and markets, and driving increased revenue. She leads with heart and spirit, and she is the perfect complement to strong leaders looking to take their businesses, and their lives, to the next level!

www.TheMariaCollins.com

ADDITIONAL RESOURCES

If you need help, or you are interested in guidance on continually growing and achieving your Dream Life, consider coaching with Maria Collins

FOR MORE INFORMATION GO TO:

www.TheMariaCollins.com

Special *FREE* Bonus Gift for You

To help you achieve success faster, get your
FREE BONUS RESOURCE at:

www.TheMariaCollins.com

Download the Fast Action Workbook that accompanies this book to help you clarify your vision, experience freedom, and live with Passion, Purpose, and Prosperity.

Made in the USA
Columbia, SC
05 November 2024